SCRAMBLES
IN THE LAKE DISTRICT

Volume 1: South

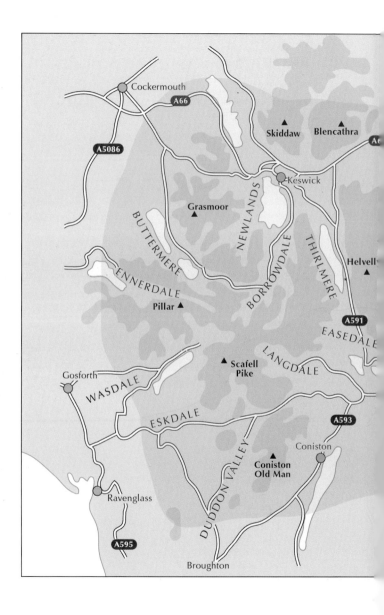

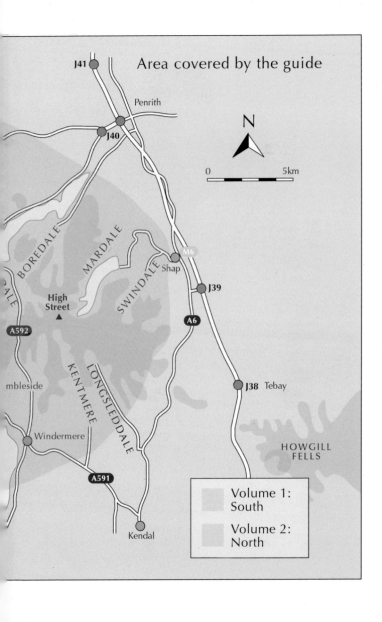

Area covered by the guide

N

0   5km

J41

Penrith

J40

M6

Shap

MARDALE

BOREDALE

...DALE

SWINDALE

High
Street ▲

A592

A6

J39

J38 Tebay

mbleside

KENTMERE

LONGSLEDDALE

Windermere

HOWGILL
FELLS

A591

Kendal

Volume 1:
South

Volume 2:
North

About the Author

Brian Evans, now retired after a career in printing and publishing, has enjoyed a lifetime's love of the outdoors. He has climbed, walked, skied and camped in many parts of Europe and North America, yet always returns to the Lake District, which has a special place in his affections. He prefers to explore out-of-the-way places, preferably with the added attraction of rock, to which he has been addicted since childhood.

Brian has always enjoyed adventure sports including pot-holing, wild-water canoeing, skiing and alpine mountaineering. He still particularly enjoys rock climbing in all its forms, from long adventurous climbs where route-finding skills are necessary to single-pitch bolted sports climbs in the Mediterranean sun. Recently, with encouragement from his grandson, he has taken up mountain biking.

Some of Brian's most memorable trips include multi-day alpine climbs such as the West face routes of the Dru and the Aiguille Noire; walking across the remote interior of Iceland; ski-backpacking in France; canoe-ing tumultuous alpine rivers; and delving deep underground in the Vercors potholes.

At home in Lancashire with his wife, Aileen, and collie, Meg, he enjoys drawing and painting, and planning the next adventurous trip.

SCRAMBLES
IN THE LAKE DISTRICT

Volume 1: South

by
R. Brian Evans

2 POLICE SQUARE, MILNTHORPE, CUMBRIA LA7 7PY
www.cicerone.co.uk

© Brian Evans 2005
© Photos Brian and Aileen Evans, unless otherwise stated.
Reprinted 2007, 2011
ISBN-13: 978 1 85284 443 1
ISBN-10: 185284 443 4
A catalogue record for this book is available from the British Library.
Printed by MCC Graphics, Spain.
Previously published in 2 vols:

Scrambles in the Lake District
© Brian Evans
First published 1982
Reprinted 1982, 1983
Revised 1985
Reprinted 1988, 1991, 1994, 1996, 1998, 2002
ISBN 0902 363 39 5

More Scrambles in the Lake District
© Brian Evans
First published 1990
Reprinted 1994, 1999
ISBN 1 85284 042 0

Cover: Dick Hogg on the upper part of Pike Howe (Route 8). *Photo: G. Dewitt*

CONTENTS

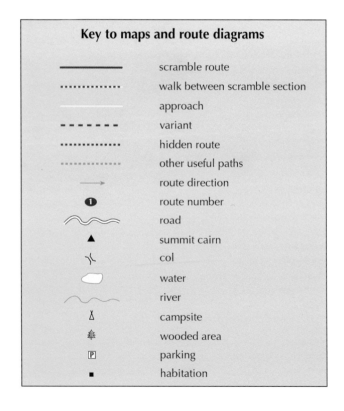

Key to maps and route diagrams

———————	scramble route
··············	walk between scramble section
——————	approach
– – – – – –	variant
••••••••••••	hidden route
················	other useful paths
—→	route direction
❶	route number
～～～	road
▲	summit cairn
⅄	col
⬭	water
～～～	river
Å	campsite
⽊	wooded area
ℙ	parking
▪	habitation

PREFACE

The first volume of *Scrambles in the Lake District* (1982) brought an enthusiastic response. The book was aimed at those with some experience of climbing and mountaineering and it opened the eyes of many people to the adventurous possibilities that exist in the Lake District. Rock climbers found that scrambling allowed them to salvage something out of a poor day, and the routes were sometimes more than enough to set the adrenalin flowing. Other people found that scrambling changed their concept of a day's fell walking. The second volume, *More Scrambles in the Lake District*, which followed in 1990 also included many memorable routes.

This new edition combines the two books into *Volume 1: South* and *Volume 2: North*. Some new routes are included, some of the less popular discarded, whilst the addition of an extra grade 4 helps to distinguish the more extreme routes.

ACKNOWLEDGEMENTS

My thanks are due to all those people who told me about their favourite scrambles. Special thanks go to Lake District artist Jim Riley, whose fell wanderings are rarely straightforward; if there is rock around, Jim has climbed it. Geoff Dewitt also deserves particular thanks. After enjoying most of the routes in the first *Scrambles* guide, Geoff and his companions Maurice Tedd and Dick Hogg embarked on a systematic appraisal of other scrambling possibilities in the Lake District. Geoff's notes, comments and photographs have proved an invaluable aid in the production of this and earlier guides. All my scrambling companions have contributed to the books, especially John Riding and the late Albert Riding, but most of all my wife Aileen. Her patience and help with the photography have been outstanding. Harry Griffin's books have been an inspiration, particularly his *Adventuring in Lakeland*, which briefly mentions many of the routes in this guide. Peter Davies of the Cumbria Raptor Study Group and Karen Slater of English Nature have both helped in bringing attention to conservation and environmental issues in this latest edition.

Brian Evans

The top of Belles Knott (Route 44) catches the late afternoon winter sun

Scrambling is a popular and rewarding pastime if the following safety code is adhered to. If the code is ignored then you could get into dangerous and possibly lethal situations: unroped scrambling in exposed situations is one of the most dangerous mountaineering practices.

- **Unroped scramblers must not slip!** Take care always to have a good hand-hold or foot-hold. Take care that your hand-hold is sound.
- **An easy, adventurous scramble in dry conditions can be transformed in wet or damp conditions into a potentially lethal misadventure.** Retreat before conditions or difficulties render the trip too hazardous.
- **Keep well within your limits.** Do not ascend where you may be unable to descend. On craglets interspersed with steep grass it is easy for the inexperienced to push into a situation where ascent is dangerous and retreat frightening.
- **A safety rope MUST be carried in the party.** This may be used to safeguard anyone who needs assurance and could be used to rescue anyone in difficulties or off-route.
- **The only relatively safe way to do an exposed grade 2, 3 or 4 scramble is as a roped climb, using belays and running belays.** Unroped scrambling on grade 2, 3 or 4 routes is only for the experienced climber/scrambler.
- **Learn how to use your rope and belays.**
- **Use a helmet when necessary.**
- **In gills expect the holds to be slippery.** Use socks over your footwear to get a better grip. Ensure that your holds are adequate to combat the slippery rock.
- **Think twice before taking children on scrambles.** They often possess neither fear nor judgement. They should be roped at all times and there should be a ratio of two adults to one child.
- **Make sure everyone in a scrambling party is aware of the dangers.**
- **Do not underestimate the seriousness of scrambling.**
- **Be aware of conservation issues** and do your best to minimise your impact on the environment.
- **A safe scrambler is someone with a background of mountaineering experience who can cope with rock-climbing situations, loose or slippery rock, has a cautious approach and is not afraid of deciding that conditions render an expedition unsafe.**
- **Please read and heed the introductory notes in guidebooks.** They are the product of experience.

Raven Crag, Yewdale, has a succession of interesting rock steps (Route 66)

INTRODUCTION

The sport of scrambling is not new. The ascent of easy rocks where hands may be used is naturally satisfying and has always been enjoyed by mountaineers, in fact the ascent of the majority of Alpine peaks by their normal route involves some scrambling. Many of the Lake District scrambles have been known since Victorian times and many have been used by generations of climbers. Early climbers created routes that involved roped scrambling without today's numerous aids to safety; high-standard rock climbing has now become so specialized that it is a sport far removed from the rock climbing of even 20 or 30 years ago, and low standard or scrambling routes are no longer relevant in a climber's guidebook full of extremes.

It is difficult to know just where to draw the line and recognise where scrambling becomes rock climbing. Some consider scrambling ends when you need a rope, but this is so much a personal choice that one person's easy scramble is another's frightening climb. I regard scrambling to be an ascent of rock where the hands are necessary for progress, usually with comforting holds. There may also be a few difficult rock moves required in order to overcome an obstacle, but scrambling means never climbing up what you can't climb down. Scramblers also need to take responsibility for their own safety and for their actions on potentially dangerous terrain, a quite different frame of mind from the modern rock climber who may feel exposed when venturing a few feet above a bolt or nut protection.

The Lake District scrambles use what the area has to offer and cannot compare with the extensive scrambling available in Skye or other

Nearing the top of Brim Fell Slabs (Route 49). Photo: B.Freed

craggier areas, so climbers expecting long, continuous rock routes may be disappointed. Do not expect rock climbs, more a series of rock incidents in a day on the hills. Much is left to the individual – on many of the routes it is a simple matter to bypass most of the rock and reduce the outing to a steep walk. You can also often choose to make the route more difficult by seeking steeper rock problems. I have described in this guide what I consider to be an interesting line, which if lost need not be a calamity, for you may find an equally worthy way.

DANGERS

Scrambling is an adventure sport, which implies that it is dangerous.

Dow Crag from Goat's Water (Routes 79–82)

Part of the attraction of any adventure sport lies in safely overcoming potential hazards, and when scrambling this means not slipping. Unlike modern rock climbing, which is steep and generally well protected, a fall whilst scrambling, which is generally unprotected, can be very serious. You must return to the maxim followed by rock climbers before the advent of modern gear – **YOU MUST NOT SLIP**.

Scrambling involves ascending rock that is not usually of sustained difficulty nor steep enough to warrant the use of what are termed 'rock-climbing' skills. However, a word of warning: although, with care, the easier scrambles are quite within the capabilities of a wide range of people, it is worth remembering that **unroped scrambling in exposed situations is potentially the most dangerous of all mountaineering situations**.

On the more difficult scrambles the exposure is often dramatic, and it is advisable to take a rope for safety. Persons tackling these should have experience of rock climbing and the necessary belay and rope techniques to allow a safe ascent or retreat. Good judgement is needed to attempt the routes in bad weather, but an experienced climber should know just how far he or she can go on wet or greasy rock and know when to retreat. **Adventurous walkers who are using this book should tackle the easiest routes only in good conditions**. It is inadvisable to venture on them at all in wintry conditions, as a thin coating of ice over the easiest rocks

can create an impossible and dangerous hazard. Snow and ice will turn most of the routes into serious and difficult winter climbs.

The rewards are great and the penalties severe. A recommended book, which delves into the philosophy of the subject, is Colin Mortlock's *The Adventure Alternative* (Cicerone Press). Mortlock has many thought-provoking theories and divides adventure into bands. Every individual has their adventure threshold, the boundary between intense enjoyment and command of the situation, and fear that could result in misadventure. For some individuals that threshold is quite low; others need a much more gripping situation to savour the adventure. Find your threshold and keep within your own limits.

Finally, **think twice before taking children on scrambles**. Whilst they are often natural scramblers and show little fear, they do not possess experience or sound judgement. They need constant supervision and should be roped at all times. Also, leave your dog below for the duration of the trip. Whilst it is possible to push and pull a dog up the easiest gills, it is not fair on you or it. If left to run loose, it will run round the hazards often seeking an escape up loose and vegetated side walls, sending rocks down on the party and doing damage to the environment.

To sum up, the safest scrambler is someone with a background of many years experience of mountaineering, who can cope with rock climbing

15

Scrambling on Little Blake Rigg (Route 86)

situations, loose or slippery rock, has a cautious approach and is not afraid of deciding that conditions render an expedition unsafe.

The British Mountaineering Council's participation statement should be heeded.

'The BMC recognises that climbing, hillwalking and mountaineering are activities with a danger of personal injury or death. Participants in these activities should be aware of and accept these risks and be responsible for their own actions and involvement.'

EQUIPMENT AND ROPE TECHNIQUES

When scrambling, it is recommended that you carry a rucksack, complete with all that you deem necessary – a compass, torch, some lunch, your waterproofs and a spare pair of dry socks (to put on after a gill scramble) – especially as most scrambles will be incorporated into a longer walk or a combination of scrambles. In addition, useful maps for the Lake District are the OS 1:25,000 Explorer Series, nos. OL4, OL5, OL6 and OL7. Harvey's Superwalker maps give a clearer, simpler picture of the terrain.

Comprehensive guidance on scrambling equipment and techniques can be found in *The Hillwalker's Guide to Mountaineering* by Terry Adby and Stuart Johnston (Cicerone Press). The following notes are derived from my own experience and are relevant to the particular situations encountered in the Lake District.

Useful websites are: **www.ami. org. uk** (the Association of Mountaineering Instructors) and **www.bmg.org.uk** (British Mountain Guides). Scrambling

courses are often available at the National Mountain Centres of Plas y Brenin, **www.pyb. co.uk**, and Glenmore Lodge, **www.glenmorelodge.org.uk**.

Ropes, rope work and belays

Although most scrambling is done unroped, a rope should be carried by the party and must be used when the leader deems that the less confident

A rope can be reassuring – Tarn Beck (Route 83)

needs assurance, when the route is extremely exposed (as on an open crag) or to protect a particularly difficult pitch. I use a rope that is 50m long and 9mm thick, which can be used double for short difficulties or single to protect less confident followers. For the grade 4 routes a double rope should be used, as in standard climbing practice. A thicker single rope may be preferred. You must allow a reasonable length of rope for abseiling out of difficulty.

The rope is of little use unless the party can be safely belayed to a firm anchorage. Modern safety techniques are not the prerogative of the climber, and the scrambler must learn the basics. To keep equipment to a minimum I prefer to tie directly to the rope with a bowline or figure-of-eight and use a waist belay; others may prefer the comfort of a harness. Trees or spikes may be used as anchors, but more often these are lacking and a nut belay must be inserted into a crack of a suitable width. To this end a selection of three or four varying sized nuts, tape slings and karabiners (including screwgate karabiners for belaying) should be carried in the party. One of the slings should be a long tape that can also serve as an abseil sit-sling. There is no need to clutter oneself with the excessive hardware commonly used in modern rock climbing.

Needless to say, anyone unfamiliar with the techniques required to use this equipment must study a basic rock-climbing instruction book and practice. However, do not be put

off – the placement of a firm belay is largely a matter of common sense and the rope handling requirements are quickly learned. The best way of learning is either from an experienced friend or a qualified mountain guide or instructor.

If the leader is highly competent and will not fall, the rope is there to stop the slips of less confident members of the party. Remember, a scrambling slip is more likely to result in a fall over easy-angled or broken rock than the steep free-falls of genuine rock climbing, and this means scramblers' falls are more likely to result in injury than a climber falling off a steep crag.

Helmets

Wearing a helmet is undoubtedly safer but many people accept the risk and go without one. However, modern helmets are so light that there is no reason to avoid using one. If a rope is used, again take care that it does not flick any loose stones onto those below.

Footwear

Scrambling is usually done in boots or all-terrain footwear that have a semi-stiff sole and narrow welt. The best have some lateral rigidity in the sole – good quality approach shoes are a popular choice. Avoid dangerous, cheap bendy boots sold in many non-specialist shops and instead choose your boots carefully; secure footwear is a vital safety factor. It may be tempting to use specialist rock boots, but smooth soles are dangerous on grass,

Socks worn over footwear provide a better grip in slippery gills

which is often encountered on a scramble. Socks (preferably old woollen ones) over the top of approach shoes can be useful in certain circumstances, particularly in a greasy gill. Trainers are not recommended although some people find it easier to take socks over the top of them than boots. If this is the case, trainers should be used as an additional aid and not as a substitute for boots.

First aid kit

Someone in the party should carry and know how to use a first aid kit in order to deal with any minor injury. In case of major accidents that require assistance from Mountain Rescue, use the nearest telephone or a mobile (if there is an adequate signal). Dial 999 and ask for the police.

Foot-holds

When scrambling the most basic requirement is to ascend rock without either slipping or pulling the holds away. In the gills slippery rock is a natural hazard, varying in degree according to location. Always expect your foot to slip if placed on a sloping hold, so ensure that your hand-holds are sufficient that you can regain control if you do slip. In these slippery gill beds, place the boot between rocks so that the boot will tighten its hold if it slips. Use sharp-edged foot-holds, even if they are smaller than more obvious slippery sloping ones. If the pitch is obviously slippery then either take boots off and proceed in socks, or put socks over trainers brought specifically for the purpose (remember

19

that trainers are bendier than boots and will not be as secure on small holds). Be aware that socks wear through!

Easy-angled waterslides pose few problems to climbers used to balance climbing, which relies on foot-holds,

Pussie's Paradise (Route 67) has a difficult start, which can be avoided on the left

with hands low to assist balance. Novice climbers tend to reach ever higher for non-existent jug hand-holds, which makes a slip more probable as the weight of the body is transferred from a vertical position (which helps to hold the foot in place) to a position almost parallel to the slabs (which helps to push the foot off the hold). A slip on a waterslide slab can result in a long and dangerous slide and people below can be swept off like skittles.

Hand-holds

Pulling holds away is easier than you may think, particularly in gills with loose rock or on a fault line where the basic rock structure may be shattered. If there is any possibility that a flake fingerhold may ping off, use it with caution and delicacy. Spikes may be large but insecure. Treat them with respect. Even on the best rock there are loose holds and perched blocks. Aim to avoid a sudden upset of balance. A heave and pull approach can be positively dangerous, particularly if the person is unaware of the dangers. Do not pull outwards on any hold where there is the possibility that it may become detached. Upward progress can often be made more safely by pushing rather than pulling. Knees can be useful.

Roped scrambling

In gills a short rope is necessary to safeguard occasional steep or exposed passages. Most of the scrambling will be done unroped.

On buttresses or craglets, the scrambling is much more open and exposed, route finding is important and it is easy for the inexperienced to find themselves in a situation where ascent is dangerous and retreat frightening. In these situations roped scrambling is the only relatively safe solution, coupled with sound belaying techniques. Unroped scrambling on grade 2, 3 or 4 routes is only for the very experienced climber/scrambler.

Solo scrambling

Many competent mountaineers enjoy solo scrambling, yet the dangers are many. It is so easy to stray into unforeseen difficulties where retreat is hazardous, especially if the rock is slippery. In a party someone can usually bypass the difficulty and drop a rope; alone any mistake could be costly, and a minor incident may become a major problem. Think twice about going alone – it's much more fun anyway with a companion.

TYPES OF SCRAMBLE

Crag scrambling

Some of the best scrambles in the Lake District are found on crags that are at too easy an angle or are too broken for difficult rock climbing. For scramblers, however, there is a satisfaction about weaving an intricate way up a broken buttress, searching out the most continuous rock to give a long scramble to often end close to a summit. Experienced

21

Slabs need balance climbing, with hands low – Harter Fell (Route 100)

climbers will find the crags – or cra-glets – entertaining. In practice, this often means linking suitable outcrops of rock to form a way up the hillside. Alternatively the route takes an easy way through areas of steeper crag. This type of scramble is very exposed and failure to find the correct route could be disastrous. Remember: great care is necessary to avoid a slip, and on many routes (grade 2/3/4), roped scrambling is the safest means of progression.

Gill scrambling

A dry spell, with a low water flow, is the best time for gill scrambling. There are few route-finding problems on gill scrambles; the pitches are often short and there is much less exposure than on crags. Therefore easier gills form a good introduction to scrambling. The Lake District is fortunate in possess-ing a wealth of gills which give good sport. In years of adventuring in many parts of Europe and Britain I have rarely encountered any counterparts as good as the Lakeland gills.

Gill scrambling demands self-imposed rules for maximum enjoyment. Harry Griffin has described his rules in *Adventuring in Lakeland* (Robert Hale). Basically, rule one is to take the hardest

Keep to the rocky bed of the gill to avoid damaging rare vegetation – Low Birker Force (Route 102)

route and that closest to the water, only straying from the streambed when the direct way is impassable. Rule two is to stick to the rock as much as possible, only wading – or in extreme cases, swimming – when progress by climbing is impossible. This often means performing difficult rock moves a few centimetres above a pool, or struggling to ascend a difficulty when it would be much easier to walk round. Griffin advocates a direct approach despite waterfalls and spray and even scorns the idea of doing the gills in drought. I prefer to assume that my legs will get wet but draw the line at anything else, and the gills are described here on that basis. However, water conditions are so variable that each party will probably encounter slightly different problems and have to make their own judgements.

The most serious gill scrambles, some would say the only ones worth doing, lie in ravines, which are common in the Lake District, but having sampled the delights of the clean water-washed rock, more open streams are not to be dismissed. Gills which cascade over broad belts of rock give entertaining scrambling with a choice of route and opportunity to make the ascent as difficult or as easy as you wish. Nevertheless, a rope should be carried to safeguard the occasional hazard and provide protection for anyone in the party who requires it.

Bear in mind that some of the gills are heavily vegetated and can be oppressively luxuriant in the height of summer. Midges can also prove troublesome at times. Choosing the right gill for the available conditions needs thought. When Lakeland is blighted by a pall of low-lying unmoving cloud which renders crags slippery and hill-walking unattractive, gills can be entertaining and rewarding, provided there is not too much water flowing. In a prolonged dry spell, go for those special routes which rarely come into perfect condition. These routes are in gills that normally carry a good deal of water and drain a large area. The small gills are feasible after a few days of dry weather in summer. In a period of mixed weather, when the ground remains sodden, you may find more water than you anticipated. A good gill scramble can be rendered useless if you cannot easily criss-cross the stream and use water-washed rock. Spring brings other problems. I have been thwarted, on a perfect day in a dry spell, by snow meltwater.

A dry spell in winter can give good gill scrambling, particularly as you are sheltered from the wind, but beware of ice lingering in ravines; water-splashed rock with an almost invisible veneer of ice can be hazardous. In true winter conditions some gills provide magnificent winter-climbing routes, but these are out of the scope of this guide.

GILLS AND SCRAMBLING

by Karen Slater (English Nature)

What are gills?

The term 'gill' is Scandinavian in origin and is generally associated with the Lake District and especially with the Borrowdale volcanic series, where streams exploit its weaknesses. A gill can be a relatively open small stream but usually refers to one with very steep sides and a rocky bed. The alternative spelling of 'ghyll' was coined by the Victorians and is poetic in origin, and its use correlated with the Victorians' increasing interest in and romanticism of the landscape as they took trips to admire the waterfalls within the gills – the previous boardwalk in Tilberthwaite Gill was evidence of this.

Gills are not, however, confined to the Lakes. Gorge scrambling has now extended to north Wales, where it is causing local problems, and many of the upper glens of Scotland (such as Glen Nevis and Glen Etive) have similar characteristics to the gorges of the Lakes. Abroad, similar features are found in western Norway and the Pyrenees, being associated with high humidity, but on a grander scale.

Early climbers

Early climbers originally followed the lines of weakness and naturally scrambled up the gills before gradually turning to climb the steeper gullies. Interest in the gills persisted and in the last 15 years has undergone a renewal of interest. This has been partly because of their aesthetic appeal and the freedom to move without ropes and partly because of their attractiveness for increasing the number of students from outdoor centres who can be taken out with a single instructor. There has been increasing publicity describing scrambles, and although some of these routes are on the cliffs, many of them are also up the gills. Gill scrambling has therefore been with us almost since the start of climbing and people still enjoy this activity. The routes up the gills are used either as a way up to the higher peaks or just for the pleasure of the rocks and as an end in itself.

The appeal of the gills

There is a great aesthetic appeal of the contrast between the delicate plants on the one hand and the mountain landscapes on the other. Gills are the relics of the original forest vegetation and are fragments that show what the original landscape would have been before the interference of man. It is very evocative to climb up a gill, even one as popular as Dungeon Gill, and get an impression of what the original landscape would have been like before the arrival of man. However, the gills occupy a very small area and with the precariousness of the plants clinging to the walls they are very fragile and are easily damaged by those climbing up the gill side.

The harm popularity can cause
Scrambling has caused formerly obscure places to suddenly become immensely popular and this can lead to irreversible damage. Carelessness is the main cause of the problems; apart from the damage arising from the trail of open gates, litter and broken walls, people can also harm the soft vegetation on the gill walls. The mountain gills are especially vulnerable because they have developed so far without disturbance. The last ice age left Lakeland some 10,000 years ago and in its wake waves of plants colonised the bare debris left by the retreating ice, eventually leading to rich and complex vegetation.

Groups often use the easier gills – Stickle Gill (Route 9)

What vegetation can be found in the gills today?
The first colonisers of the Lake District were alpine plants, which were resistant to cold and exposure. These were eventually replaced over much of the landscape by birch and pine, which in turn gave way to the familiar oak and ash. However, the rocky sides of the gills and the mountain summits always

remained clear of trees. The fragments of vegetation are thus similar to the mountains of the continent and the lowlands of the Arctic and Scandinavia. Forest trees filled the valleys and the hillsides up to about 520m before, gradually over the centuries, man cleared the forest and brought sheep to graze on the fells. The only refuges left for the alpine plants remaining were the protected cliffs and rocky gill sides. Such sheltered sites occupy only a tiny fraction of the land surface (less than 0.5%).

Today different groups of plants are found within the many gills – their ecological preferences determining which gill offers the best environment for them. In the lower gills there are many woodland species; **oak** and **ash** give way to **birch** and **rowan** at higher levels. Some woodland plants, such as **wood anemone** and **violet**, still manage to grow on the highest cliffs and gills, but the most common plants throughout the gills are the moorland and woodland species. A specialised group of species, including **butterwort** and **devil's-bit scabious**, is also present on ledges beside water trickles. Because of the dampness of the soil and its peaty texture careless feet and hands very easily destroy these ledges. Also growing on some ledges are plants with a preference for richer soils that are usually found in lowland meadows, such as **meadowsweet** and **globeflower**. Finally there are the special alpine species like the mossy **saxifrage** and **roseroot**; these are only found in the higher gills.

The composition of the gills thus changes with altitude as the climate and environment become more severe; here only upland species can survive. Thus only in the high-level gills that are situated 450m up on the side of Helvellyn, the Langdale Pikes and even more famously on the north side of the Scafell range will you find a few **dwarfed rowan** bushes clinging to the cliffs. The highest gill sides are bare of trees and have comparable vegetation to the Arctic.

Which gills in particular are important?

Both the **individual plant species** and **the assemblages** in which they occur are important. Many gills are within Sites of Special Scientific Interest (SSSI).

The following gills are notified as SSSIs:

- Stanley Gill
- Dungeon Gill
- Tilberthwaite Gill
- Skelghyll Beck

- Browgill
- Stockdale Becks
- Sourmilk Gill (Buttermere).

There are also gills designated SSSIs that are within wider upland/ woodland:

- Thirlmere Woods (Launchy Gill)
- Lodore and Troutdale Woods (including Watendlath Beck and Ashness Gill)
- Scafell Pikes (including Ruddy Gill, Greta Gill and Calf Cove Gill)
- Naddle Forest (including Guerness Gill)
- Helvellyn and Fairfield (including Hogget Gill)
- Great Wood (Cat Gill)
- Armboth Fells
- Skiddaw group
- Buttermere Fells
- Wasdale Screes
- Pillar and Ennerdale Fells
- Seatoller Woods (Sourmilk Gill)
- Seathwaite Graphite Mine.

A high nature conservation interest is shown in many other gills have that have not been notified as SSSI. Some examples are:

- Sandbed Gill (St Johns in the Vale)
- White Gill near Coniston
- Holbeck Gill, Troutbeck
- Atkinsons Grain near Bampton
- Combe Gill, Rosthwaite
- Middlesteads Gill, Thirlmere
- Crinkle Gill, Langdale
- Raise Gill.

When scrambling up the walls of the gills place your feet and hands carefully, avoiding damaging vegetation or even pulling off branches of trees. These impacts may destroy vegetation that may never regrow in our lifetime.

How can you help?

If we are to conserve the unique and beautiful array of plants in the gills then we have to spread quickly and widely the message that these plants are particularly sensitive to careless use.

Ensure that you
- keep to the rocky bed of the gill
- follow only established routes
- keep groups in line
- avoid crumbling rocks where many of the delicate species lie
- leave the plants for others to enjoy.

If these suggestions are followed much of the sensitive vegetation can be conserved, and we can leave for future generations the attractive plants that we ourselves enjoy today.

Please go to the gills and enjoy them: respect the plants and be aware of the surroundings and the impacts that you can have.

Bad weather scrambling

Many rock climbers use scrambles as a means of salvaging something exciting on a day of poor weather. **However, in bad conditions the crags are treacherously slippery and many climbers have got more than they bargained for**. Do not underestimate the seriousness of these routes. Remember the aspect of a crag is very important: south- and west-facing rocks are usually cleaner and quicker drying. At the onset of rain,

The broad rocky face of Ill Crag hosts one of Lakeland's best mountaineering scrambles (Route 116)

before the water has chance to build up flow, the clean water-washed rocks of a gill scramble may still offer good sport.

Exploratory scrambling

Exploratory scrambling can create some interesting and hazardous days. Most people will be content to tackle the standard good quality routes, but for the person who has done everything – that is, most of the rock climbs and scrambles within his/her grade, and most of the popular summits, scrambling where fancy takes you can be quite satisfying. However, a word of warning: if you are not careful you can easily get into some particularly nasty situations. There is an awful lot of rubbishy crag in the Lake District! The best rough rock lies in the central fells, whilst east of Thirlmere it tends

to be smoother and more vegetated. The Skiddaw Slates, which comprise all the fells north of Buttermere (except the head of Newlands), are shattered and rarely give good scrambling. One or two gills that seem promising prove slippery and the water-washed channel may be veiled with a curtain of moss (some are good winter ice-climbs but these are of no interest to the scrambler).

The pioneer rock climbers often chose gullies for their climbs, with a mistaken sense of security. I would strongly advise the scrambler to keep away from most gullies, for they are dank and desperate. Invariably the rock is slippery and even the most innocent-looking cleft has its bed blocked by chockstones which are often strenuous and serious obstacles.

Thorn Crag (Route 3) provides easy scrambling on excellent rock

Stick to the easy-angled little craglets and string them together to make an interesting ascent, or choose a pleasant open streambed to follow to the tops. Make sure you are not disturbing nesting birds and take great care not to damage the environment.

CONSERVATION AWARENESS

Concern has been expressed by conservationists and botanists that gill scrambling leads to the destruction of a sensitive habitat for rare plants and birds. The conflict of interest between the adventure-seeking scrambler and the conservationists is not an easy one to resolve. Please be aware of the problem and leave no sign of your passage. If you stick to the clean water-washed rock then no damage is inflicted on the vegetation. Once you have recourse to the side walls you could damage the vegetation.

Some of the gills are in protected SSSIs (Site of Special Scientific Interest) and should be traversed with the utmost care. Those routes that are in such areas are identified in the guide as being SSSIs or as areas of nature conservation interest (see Using this Guide below for further details).

Do not pollute the stream, it may be someone's water supply, but before taking a drink yourself, remember that ravines are often the last resting place of suicidal sheep! Some crags with nesting peregrines or ravens are subject to access restrictions in the nesting season. Details of these are available on the BMC website: **www.thebmc.co.uk.**

USING THIS GUIDE

Symbols used in the text are as follows:

⚠ = route within an SSSI (Site of Special Scientific Interest)
🌿🌿 = gill with great nature conservation interest
🌿 = gill with some nature conservation interest.

Grading
Grades are for ascents in good dry conditions. Wet rock, particularly on the crags, can increase the grade considerably or render a scramble extremely hazardous. I have introduced a grade 4 to replace the traditional 3S, which denoted an especially serious route. All scrambling is serious.

Grade 1 is a straightforward scramble, with little or no route-finding difficulty. The described route takes the most interesting line, which can usually be varied or even avoided at will. Generally, the exposure is not great, but even so, great care must be taken to avoid a slip.

Grade 2 contains longer and more difficult stretches of scrambling, and a rope may be useful for ensuring safety in the more exposed passages. Although individual sections of the scramble can usually be avoided, these sections may be inescapable once the scramble is underway. Some skill in route finding is required to follow the described line.

Grade 3 is a more serious proposition, only to be undertaken by competent parties. Escape is difficult. A rope is advisable for safety on exposed passages and for some pitches of easy rock climbing. The routes require a steady leader with the ability to judge how the rest of the party are coping with the situations, and a rope should be used wherever the safety of an individual is in doubt.

Grade 4 denotes a particularly serious outing, perhaps containing very exposed passages on steep rock, poor rock or vegetation. Recommended only for experienced, competent climbers who will almost certainly use a rope on key pitches. Escape is difficult. This supersedes the 3S grade used in previous guides (many of the lower graded routes are still serious propositions).

Note that grade 3 and 4 routes, particularly in gills, may include moves which would merit up to a 'v diff' grading in rock-climbing guides.

Many of the routes described follow what I consider to be the most rewarding route for continuity and interest. This often involves scrambling over rock outcrops, which could be easily avoided by a short detour (thus reducing the grading with the consequent loss of interest). So much is up to the choice of the individual. Rock climbers will doubtless choose their own lines to suit their chosen standard or use the scrambles as a variation of 'bouldering'.

The star system
This gives a useful indication of quality. **One star** (∗) represents a route, which although not classic, has its good points and is worthy of attention. **Two stars** (∗∗) represent a route of more continuous interest and a good line, whilst **three stars** (∗∗∗) are reserved for classic routes with more continuously interesting scrambling that is based on a good line.

THE ROUTES

The scrambles are described valley by valley beginning with popular Langdale. The map reference refers to the approximate start of each route. Right and left means in the direction of travel. The height of a route is the vertical height gain and will include a mixture of rock scrambling and walking.

Very few of the routes as described are suitable for descent; but some can be descended close to the described route if you choose easier alternatives on grassy rakes. Generally, an ascent is so much more worthwhile that it is best to plan an itinerary combining several ascents, rather than lose interest in an unsatisfactory descent. When looking up a rocky buttress the continuous scrambling is obvious. When looking down, there often appears to be a surfeit of grass and it is difficult to choose a continuous rock descent.

Jack's Rake (Route 16) levels between scrambling sections

ACCESS, CONSERVATION AND BIRD RESTRICTIONS

by Kevin Howett and Peter Davies
(Chairman of the Cumbria Raptor Study Group)

Reproduced with permission of the Fell and Rock Climbing Club

Access and conservation

Access to the crags of the Lake District is taken for granted by the majority of visitors but in fact in some cases access may have been achieved only through years of patient negotiation. Fortunately, the **National Trust**, **Forestry Commission**, **United Utilities** and other private owners who are broadly sympathetic to climbers own most of the Lakeland crags. In a few cases, however, the situation remains delicate and increasing numbers of climbers or scramblers are only likely to make it more so. This is an area in which we can all help, not only by cherishing this region in the manner it deserves – parking thoughtfully, co-operating with farmers and landowners, following the country code, observing bird restrictions, picking up litter at crags and so on – but by ensuring that others do the same. Outsiders look on climbers as a group, and inconsiderate behaviour by a few will be seen, rightly or wrongly, as a reflection upon us all. The onus is on all of us to make certain that it doesn't happen in the first place.

Bird restrictions

Several of the Lake District crags carry **bird restrictions** in the spring (typically from 1st March to 30th June). However, the situation changes from year to year and climbers should make efforts beforehand to find out if there are Schedule 1 birds or ravens in residence on the crag they intend to visit. Usually restricted crags will be signed, but this may not always be the case, and all climbers or scramblers should acquaint themselves with the latest known details which can be found on the BMC website at **www.thebmc. co.uk** or on the FRCC website at **www.frcc.co.uk/rock/ birds.htm**. Where birds have not nested in any particular year, the ban may be lifted earlier. If there are birds nesting, and there is an agreed restriction, then please be prepared to change your plans according to the agreement. It may be that only some parts of the crag are restricted, so other routes can be climbed. If this is the case it will be indicated on the signs. The notes below have been drawn up jointly by the Lake District National Park Authority, the

National Trust, the Cumbria Raptor Study Group, English Nature, The British Mountaineering Council Area Committee and the Fell and Rock Climbing Club. They are intended to cover only the Lake District and outlying areas of Cumbria, though they may be found useful elsewhere.

All birds and their eggs and nests are protected by the **Wildlife and Countryside Act 1981**. Certain rare or more endangered species are further protected by increased penalties under the 1981 act and must not be intentionally or recklessly disturbed when nesting. These birds are listed in the act and are referred to as Schedule 1 species. Many are ground-nesting or tree-nesting birds, some are found on sea cliffs, but the Schedule 1 bird species that climbers may most commonly encounter on crags in the Lake District is the peregrine falcon. Some agreed restrictions also apply to ravens (though these are not Schedule 1).

Peregrines

Peregrines are the largest falcons in the British Isles. They can be recognized by their distinctive profile, often sighted from the crag, as they plummet groundwards to seize some unsuspecting prey. Seen from below, they are pale-coloured birds with dark tips to the tail and wings. Their call is a piercing shriek, once heard never forgotten, particularly if you are leading at the time! When the peregrine is disturbed this is uttered repeatedly for long periods. Peregrines hunt over a variety of habitats catching medium-sized birds, mainly feral pigeons, by swooping at speeds of up to 200km an hour to seize them. The optimum and preferred nesting sites of peregrines in the United Kingdom are rocky coastal areas, cliffs and inland crags, but the actual nest site is not at all obvious, being just a shallow scrape in the soil. Some indication may be given by streaks of white guano (bird droppings) down an area of the crag, though this may merely be a roost site for the male rather than a nest.

Peregrines are fairly common in the Lake District which is one of their most important European habitats, but they are rare elsewhere. In fact the United Kingdom supports approximately 14% of the European population. Of these, in Cumbria, there are usually about 85 nesting sites which hold one or more birds each year and approximately 65 pairs attempt to breed each season. This is 6% of the UK's total population and is considered to be the densest breeding population in the world. The Cumbrian birds are especially important because of the population numbers and productivity which is enabling the birds to spread and re-colonise other areas in the

UK. They are particularly vulnerable to the weather, disturbance, poor food supply and illegal activities such as shooting, poisoning, and egg and chick theft. In 2000 there were 83 occupied territories on which 46 pairs reared 111 young. However, in 2002 only 32 young were reared and this was the worst recorded breeding season for 30 years, predominantly due to appalling weather, but also to increased robberies. Climbers can assist here by reporting any suspicious characters they see near peregrine nest sites.

Ravens
Ravens are very large black birds, similar to a rook but a third bigger. They have distinctive deep 'pruk-pruk' and 'grok' calls and are great aerial acrobats that delight in soaring and tumbling. Ravens, while not protected in the same way as peregrines and eagles, are still under potential threat from increased disturbance, and there are some voluntary restrictions in the Lake District on their account. Their nests are very large piles of twigs.

Bird Restrictions Agreements
Bird Restrictions are agreed annually between the local BMC Area Committee, the National Park Authority and English Nature. The area of crag agreed to be avoided can vary depending upon various factors including the layout of the crag. Some pairs also vary their choice of nesting site each year either within a crag or between different crags and so agreements may change from year to year. In general, they only apply to the most popular rock-climbing crags but this does not mean that people are necessarily allowed to climb or scramble on all other crags during this period; even where a crag is not subject to a restriction, if you suspect a bird (particularly a peregrine) is nesting on it, you should heed the advice below. Areas where birds are known to nest should be avoided for a period running from the 1st March to 30th June in the case of the peregrine, and from 1st March to 31st May for the raven.

How the law affects you
The law states that it is an offence to 'intentionally' or 'recklessly' disturb a Schedule 1 bird 'at, on or near' the nest. It is also an offence to recklessly or intentionally disturb 'dependent' fledged young. These fledglings are young birds that have just moved away from the nest but are still dependent to some extent on their parents for food and protection.

It is clear and unambiguous what 'at' and 'on' mean in this legislation, but the law does not stipulate a definition for 'near'. Nor does the law stipulate what constitutes 'disturbance'. It would be difficult to do this, as each bird species is different, and indeed individual birds are different. As a result, the prosecution would call upon expert witnesses to testify that disturbance occurred. It would also have to be shown that it was intentional or reckless.

Many peregrine falcon sites are monitored under licence by **Raptor Study Groups**, and it is important that scramblers follow some basic guidance in order to minimise disturbance (and allow both birds and scramblers to continue to coexist) as well as to make sure they are not breaking the law. Apart from possible prosecution, if you are arrested police can confiscate your climbing equipment as evidence to present at the trial, and the case may take a long time to come to court.

The following information will give a basic knowledge of Schedule 1 bird behaviour for scramblers to judge for themselves what action to take. It is not intended to be definitive, but to be a general guide.

A step down into the gill near the top of Tarn Beck (Route 83). Scramblers need to be aware of disturbance to nesting birds and retreat if neccessary.

At the crag

If you visit a crag not listed as having an agreement, but then notice activity from a peregrine or other Schedule 1 bird in the vicinity, then the guidance below will help you decide what to do. It can equally be used for some other nesting birds you may come across, such as ravens. Obviously, your choice of what can be done will depend on the extent of the crag and its topography as well as other factors outlined below.

As you walk into the crag keep a look out for peregrines and other birds. Peregrines in particular may be calling as they fly about the area. When you arrive they may be disturbed but this is quite normal intuitive disturbance. Try and move out of their line of sight as quickly as you can and then wait and see if they settle down, and then try to spot where they originate. This will enable you to decide whether there is a nesting site that is being used near the route that you are hoping to do and to assess from the disturbance criteria below whether you feel your presence will be detrimental to the birds.

If the nest site is not directly beside where you are going to climb, if the configuration of the crag means you can be separated from line of sight from the nest site to some extent or if the crucial period of egg incubation (see below) in cold weather is past, you will probably find that the birds will have calmed down after the initial disturbance and that your climbing does not disturb them off the nest for long periods.

If the birds continue to appear aggressive and agitated and are staying away from the nest, you should find another route further away from the site, on another part of the crag, or indeed another crag. To continue climbing could keep the parents off the nest for too long so causing damaging disturbance.

How do you judge disturbance?

Most birds will act instinctively to protect their nest site when they perceive a threat. They will often make an initial reaction to human presence by calling, often repeatedly or aggressively. They will then either realise there is no threat and will settle down or, if they continue and you then move away from them, they will stop their instinctive behaviour.

It can be difficult for non-ornithologists to judge when a peregrine's call changes from normal activity to that of a protection call, but listen for a more aggressive tone. If the female then flies from the nest and stays away, then they have been disturbed and it becomes detrimental to breeding success.

How close is too close?

There are no hard and fast rules to determine when you might be too close as so much depends upon the tolerance of the individual bird. If the crag is very popular with climbers or scramblers, any nesting birds may be habituated to the presence of climbers. Such peregrines may be able to accept climbing in quite close proximity, as long as it is around the other side of an arête or on a separate buttress. One thing that you can be sure of is that climbing very close or directly onto the nest will cause damaging disturbance. At crags in remote areas where there is little climbing activity birds may be disturbed even at some distance. Of particular importance is the line of sight. If the bird can see you it is far more likely to be disturbed. The best policy is to err upon the side of caution, and if in any doubt retreat.

The most important period of nesting

For most birds the most sensitive periods are up to the time they lay their eggs, and when they have just laid eggs; for peregrines this period can be from February to late April when the ambient air temperature is still low. A later sensitive period is when the chicks have just hatched (for peregrines, mid- to end of May). If adults are repeatedly or continually kept off the nest by climbers the eggs or chicks will quickly cool and die, or become available to predation. Obviously there is an even greater risk in cold conditions, and the position of the nest (on a north- or south-facing crag) and the time of day will also be important factors to take into account. For ravens, the period from mid-April to mid-May when they are feeding their chicks is critical as this process needs to be constant throughout the day or the chicks will starve.

What to do if challenged or arrested

Even with the best of intentions it is possible that, having obeyed the above guidelines, you may be accused of disturbing a bird, or of climbing on a crag where you should not have done. If asked to leave please do so without fuss, but please ask and note the name of the person requesting you to leave, the organisation they represent, and the reason you have been asked to leave. If the worst happens and you are arrested, as soon as possible make full notes of the circumstances leading up to your arrest with especial detail on the position of any nests vis-à-vis your climb and the behaviour of any birds. These notes will form vital evidence if the case goes to court, which may be months or even years after the event. In all circumstances please report the details to the **BMC**.

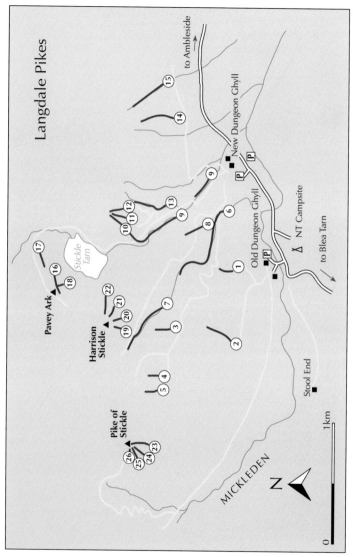

Langdale Pikes

LANGDALE

Langdale is one of Lakeland's most popular and easily accessible valleys, and is fortunate to possess a wealth of excellent scrambling. There are gills, a classic rake and crags, with many possibilities for combinations to provide ascents mainly on rock for a major part of a mountain day. Routes often culminate on or very close to a summit.

The most significant reason for this good scrambling is that much of the best rocks face into the sun, which always leads to cleaner rock. The rock is usually of excellent quality with a surfeit of solid holds and rugosities which inspire confidence (although, as on many scrambling routes, you are likely to encounter occasional loose flakes and perched blocks). Friction is generally good.

The familiar distinctive outline of the Langdale Pikes and of Pavey Ark beckon and in this small area is found some of Lakeland's best scrambling rock. At the head of the valley Bowfell presents a steep north-western face, but suffers from its aspect. Crinkle Crags is scored by several enticing gills and the rocky flanks of Pike of Blisco complete the cirque.

There are campsites at Baysbrown near Chapel Stile, and a popular National Trust site close to the Old Dungeon Ghyll Hotel.

The Langdale Pikes from Side Pike (Route 41)

Car parking and transport

Langdale is extremely popular and the parking spaces fill quickly. There is a small car park at the Old Dungeon Ghyll and a much bigger one, Stickle Gill, at the New Dungeon Ghyll. A bus service runs from Ambleside to the Old DG but the last bus back is inconveniently early for most scramblers.

1. Raven Crag

Grade 2* (on the first section) NY285064

The short crucial passage is very exposed and polished; it is followed by a mixture of airy walking and scrambling on scattered rock outcrops with about 200m vertical height gain.

Raven Crag is a very popular climbers' crag above the Old Dungeon Ghyll Hotel at the head of Langdale. A route up the craggy hillside above Raven Crag is just one of the many scramble approaches which can be used to gain height with interest to reach better things. Our route incorporates the climbers' descent path and continues up broken rocks above for a considerable distance.

Approach: From the car park at the ODG take the Mickleden track behind the hotel then go right over a

Raven Crag, Langdale and White Crag

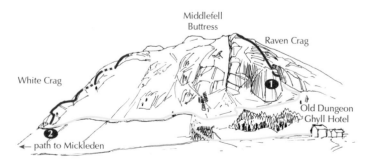

stile, through a plantation and up a well-constructed path, zigzagging under the crag and up its right-hand side into a gully.

Route: The path up the gully leads well up the side of the crags to a ledge, which leads left into the crag below a final, steep wall. Traverse this exposed ledge past some large split blocks (which are awkward to negotiate with a large ruck-sack) until you can ascend steeply from the top of a pin-nacle, or by a groove on its left, to a large grass shelf on top of the climbing crag. Above rise a series of steep walls and grass terraces. The route can be varied at will, and good rock in airy situations are linked for a considerable way until the angle eases and more walking follows to a steeper knoll which gives a scramble up the front. A main path (Dungeon Ghyll–Pikes) is crossed and the easy scrambling continues up a rocky spur to the top of a knoll. This is a fine viewpoint (as shown in the diagram Route 3) from which your continuation scrambles can be seen.

2. White Crag

Grade 2 or 3 NY281064

Well to the left of Raven Crag are a succession of out-crops that give an interesting scramble.

Approach: From the car park at the ODG take the Mickleden track behind the hotel then go right over a stile, through a plantation and up a laid path. Where this goes right under Raven Crag a slight path leads left to a stile at the top of the wall. Follow the wall left to reach the lowest rocks of White Crag.

Route: On the right of the steep, lowest wall, scram-ble to a grass ledge just left of a tree. Go left then up behind a flake to reach the crest of the buttress, which is climbed to the top of the first section. (There is a more

A linkage of outcrops of good rock, **but take great care with some loose flakes**. 200m of scrambling and walking.

43

difficult grade 3 start which takes **Bumble Arête**. This climbs the easier angled arête between the two steep crags above the wall, starting from its slabby left side.) On the right is a clean slabby rib of rock, difficult at its foot and best entered from the left about 12m from the base. The front of the rib then leads to a terrace. Cross scree on the right to the left end of a crag with a distinctive pinnacle. Scramble leftwards towards a birch, exit a recess on the left, taking care with loose blocks to a point just below the tree. Move right and up slabs on the front, to the top of a flake above the tree. Continue just right of the rib avoiding perched blocks. Enter a tiny, rocky streambed then continue up several steep little outcrops to the path below Thorn Crag.

Thorn Crag (Route 3) is the logical continuation, thence walk round the head of Dungeon Ghyll to the scrambles on Harrison Stickle (Routes 19–22) or along the crest over Loft Crag to Pike of Stickle (Routes 23–26). Alternatively one can take an almost horizontal path to the scramble on Loft Crag Buttress (Route 4).

3. Thorn Crag
Grade 1 or 2✱ NY281069

Thorn Crag

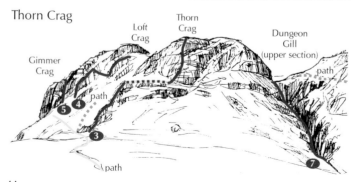

Thorn Crag provides easy scrambling on excellent rock

Approach: Via Route 1 or 2 or the footpath from the New Dungeon Ghyll (large car park) on the left of the Dungeon Ghyll. The path comes close to a rock spur at a small ruin.

Route: Ascend the rock spur above the ruin to grass slopes. Walk left to more continuous rock and up to a terrace below the crags which form the upper part of the buttress. At the lowest rocks on the right edge climb slabs, steeper at the top but well furnished with holds.

The choice now is to walk round the head of Dungeon Ghyll to Harrison Stickle, continue along the crest of the Pikes or descend slightly to reach Loft Crag.

Easy pleasant scrambling on perfect rock, exposed on the upper 100m.

4. Loft Crag Buttress

Grade 2✱ NY279069

Close to Gimmer Crag is an easier angled buttress which is suitable for scrambling. This is well to the left of the track that comes from the New Dungeon Ghyll, passes below Thorn Crag and mounts to a gap in the ridge.

Pleasant scrambling on good rock, worth incorporating into a day's sport. The route offers about 100m of scrambling.

Approach: Leave the path below the gap in the ridge and cross steep slopes to the foot of the rocks. Gimmer Crag presents a steep, bold face with a square-cut gully on its right. The right wall of this is another climbing buttress, then you find a grassy depression and finally a more amenable broken buttress. At the foot of this is a rock finger.

Route: Start just right of the finger and gain a ledge above it on top of a steep wall. Up the steep front is a system of ledges, first slanting left then back right to the edge of a rock slab. Ascend the slab edge to a terrace. On the right is a cleft leading to a parallel rock rib. Climb just to the right of the cleft to a grass ledge and slabs which turn into easy ground. Cross the scree shoot on the right to an adjacent rib. Start on its right and after a steep step follow easy-angled rock up the crest for a good finish. The summit block of Loft Crag is just above and can be scrambled up on the right.

5. South-East Gully, Gimmer

Grade 2✱ NY278069

This is a scramble of around 60m, but it is a climbers' descent route and dislodged stones could pose a danger to scramblers. **Helmet advised.**

This is the deep, square-cut gully which bounds the face of Gimmer Crag on its right. It is less used since the introduction of a climbers' abseil station, so it could be worth incorporating into a day's scrambling, particularly for the impressive rock scenery around it.

Approach: Gain the path below Thorn Crag either from the Stickle Gill NT car park by way of the Langdale Pikes path which crosses to the left side of Dungeon Gill, or by the scramble on Raven Crag. Where the main path rises onto the ridge crest between Thorn and Loft Crag a lesser path traverses the shelf towards Gimmer Crag. The gully is an obvious cleft to the right of the main face. See diagram, Route 3.

Route: Start at the right-hand corner and scramble a series of walls and ledges. Cross a central rib to gain the narrow cleft on the left. This needs care as there is loose rock and a steep, difficult finish.

6. Dungeon Ghyll, Lower Section

Grade 1✳ NY290065 🗻 ♥♥

This popular ravine provides a scenic route to the tops or other adjacent scrambles. The route splits into distinct halves, the lower being practicable in most water levels, whilst the upper ravine (Route 7) is best in dry conditions.

Approach: From Stickle Gill (New Dungeon Ghyll) car park follow the path towards Stickle Gill but almost immediately turn left to a gap in the wall on the skyline. Turn right, go over a stile to reach the stream of Dungeon Ghyll. Alternatively, a more direct path starts at the left side near the entrance to the car park.

Route: The first ravine is just above the point where the path crosses the stream and contains the impressive hidden waterfall described by William Wordsworth in his poem *The Idle Shepherd Boys*. This is worth a close look so scramble into the ravine to the foot of the 20m fall imprisoned between dark vertical walls and capped by a natural boulder bridge. Retrace your steps and escape up the left wall (looking upstream) to gain the path at the side of the gill.

Now either follow the path a short way or, if you want the spice of adventure, make the exposed crossing of the bridge (rope advised for security). This is easy but very airy, well described in Wordsworth's poem. Then keep to the right side of the gill as the bed contains several small unclimbable falls. Regain the stream just before the main path enters from the left. Follow the gill and climb the first water chute by rocks on its right. The fall above may be

The gill is more a walk than a scramble, apart from the crossing of the impressive boulder bridge and the route up the final ravine. Good waterfall scenery. About 200m is gained in height.

Stickle Gill Area

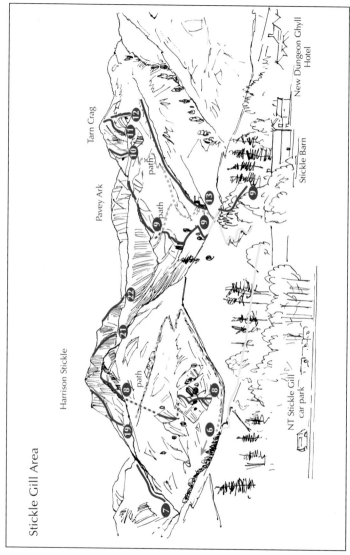

possible in drought but can be easily avoided. The ravine widens and is followed gently into the next ravine.

The second ravine is topped by a pretty cascade, which is avoided on the left. Then head back right into a scenic stretch of small falls and cascades followed by a chaos of boulders. The most sporting way keeps close to the stream. Note another boulder bridge near the top. The path leads into an impressive amphitheatre with a fine waterfall at its head.

The 15m fall is not the impasse it appears, as an easy scramble into a side gully on the left rounds the obstacle. Do not follow a path up a ramp on the right-hand side of the upper half of this gully, as it is loose and unpleasant. Instead, escape onto the grassy slope on the left. Above, the ravine opens into grassy moorland with fine views of Harrison Stickle. In all but very dry conditions it is best to leave the stream here and go to other scrambles.

7. Dungeon Ghyll, Upper Ravine
Grade 3 NY282070* 🏔 ♣ ♣

A complete contrast to the lower ravine, this has a more serious atmosphere as the walls are closer and the rock more shattered – the scrambler begins to feel that the gill is well named.

Approach: The ravine is sandwiched between Harrison Stickle and Thorn Crag and can be accessed from the paths on either side of the lower ravine, or across the moor from Stickle Tarn.

Route: Ascend the rough boulder bed of rich red stones between high, vegetated walls to the main obstacle, where the stream drops over a vertical fall in a narrow slit then cascades down a slanting trough to the boulder bed. By-pass this obstacle by going up a steep loose chimney on the right. Rope advised. Start the climb from the foot of

Be aware of walkers on the path above, for their carelessly dislodged stones may fall into the ravine. **Helmets advised.** The key passage is best surmounted in a dry spell. You will gain 100m of height.

the slanting trough and ascend steeply on good holds to an easing in angle in the gully below some chockstones, about 20m from the base. Do not ascend further as this leads out of the gill, but traverse left to reach a ledge which drops back into the stream at the top of the fall. This pitch is quite serious. Continue up the bed of the ravine past a large chockstone which could prove impassable in high water, to reach a wide amphitheatre. An escape is possible up the scree but the most interesting way is up the gill. The stream falls over the steep left wall. Climb a shattered overflow channel 7m right to a slanting ledge which crosses the next fall. Above the ledge exit directly up the short steep spout, and an easy cascade ends the scramble.

Good continuation routes are found on the south-west face of Harrison Stickle (Route 19), only a couple of minutes' walk down the path above the ravine; or cross over the intervening ridge to reach the scramble on Loft Crag Buttress (Route 4).

8. Pike Howe

Grade 2 NY291066

Discontinuous but with pleasant individual rock sections. The 180m of height gain includes some walking.

This provides another way to gain height at the start of a day. The route uses a succession of outcrops between Stickle Gill and Dungeon Ghyll.

Approach: From the Stickle Gill car park follow the path left to Dungeon Ghyll. Through a gate, above the path, is a horseshoe shaped outcrop sporting several holly bushes. Start at the lowest point of the left-hand prong of the horseshoe.

Route: From the bottom of the first outcrop climb a slabby rib, or the slab 10m to the left, to below a holly tree. Move left below the small central holly and climb the clean slabs on the right onto a rib followed by broken

rocks to the top of the first tier. Move left about 75m to climb the right rib of another outcrop. Cross the paved track (this could be followed to the final rocks if bracken

On the lower section of Pike Howe

is a problem). A few short rock steps and steep walking lead to the summit rocks. Move left to the flank overlooking Dungeon Ghyll. You can scramble in many places, but perhaps the best rock is found at the far left end close to the path; here three successive steps of good quality rock lead to the top. The final step is good on the left of the centre, and has excellent holds.

Harrison Stickle lies straight ahead with its enticing choice of scrambles (Routes 19–22), or a path right goes to Stickle Tarn and Pavey Ark (Routes 16–18).

9. Stickle (Mill) Gill

Grade 1★★ NY294066

An open gill with good clean rock. Popular for youngsters and novices who may need a rope for one steep step. There is around 200m of height gain to the foot of Tarn Crag.

The path up the side of Stickle Gill provides the most popular way to Stickle Tarn and Pavey Ark. The gill makes a sporting alternative which, with the continuation of Jack's Rake, is the most used scramble in the Lake District. Scrambling in the first part of the gill is not allowed during lambing time in April and May.

Approach: From the Stickle Gill car park a path runs up the valley by the side of the stream. It is possible to follow the gill almost from the start, or walk up the path, cross the footbridge, passing a wire fence and stile to where a path forks left into the gill. See diagram, Route 7.

Route: The first part of the tree-lined lower section starts with a steep ascent between two small falls, before a tricky traverse on the right wall. Pools and easy steps in a good rock bed make progress interesting. Above the footbridge there is a small rock step then a steeper one, which is best climbed in its cleaner centre at a rib. Novices will need to be roped for this.

Traverse a pool on its right to enter a cleft, passable in low water with bridging past boulders. Otherwise go

Stickle Gill, the first steep barrier

left to the side of a steep nose. Climb the left of this and move right onto the slabby crest. Soon the main cascades are reached. These are climbed easily on the right (excellent rock) to a junction with the path at a shelf. Join the path to reach an easy-angled rock spur on the right. If the most continuous rock is sought this makes a good way to reach Tarn Crag. Ascend to a terrace where a gangway slants right. Continue to steeper rocks and climb to the foot of a rib. Cross to the more continuous rib on the right and follow it to a shelf below the left-hand side of Tarn Crag.

Continue by any of the following routes: East Rib is possibly the best, or walk left on a path which mounts the rocky right-hand side of Stickle Gill to reach Stickle Tarn.

TARN CRAG

This broken crag lies on the right-hand side of Stickle Gill and can be approached directly via the zigzags of a paved track which branches right from the main path not far above the footbridge, or with more interest via Route 9. There are two main buttresses on either side of a central bay that are used by rock climbers. The scrambles lie to the left and right on easier angled terrain and give around 50m of height.

10. The Groove, Tarn Crag

Grade 3✷ NY290073

An awkward start up a prominent groove eases to an open buttress with some steep rock. Take care with route finding.

Route: Start 6m right of a holly bush at the foot of the main rocks, where a left slanting groove with a prominent white mark gives awkward and fairly steep climbing to a ledge. Move left up grass and back right to easy rocks. The buttress is now broad and presents plenty of choice; best keep right to achieve the longest scramble.

Tarn Crag, above the Stickle Gill path

Tarn Crag

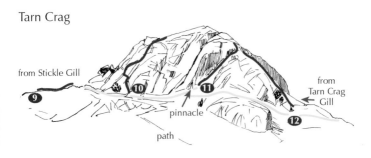

from Stickle Gill

9

10

11

pinnacle

path

from
Tarn Crag
Gill

12

11. The Spur, Tarn Crag
Grade 2∗ NY291073

Route: Walk under the crag past the central bay to a fine spur with a pinnacle at its foot. Go behind the pinnacle

*On The Spur of
Tarn Crag*

The most logical continuation from Stickle Gill (Route 9), just a little more difficult near the start, but **care is needed with doubtful flakes**.

and cross at the same level to reach the crest of an easier angled spur on the right, just below a small battered yew. Make a short traverse right, just below the yew, to an awkward exposed ascent past it. Follow the rib for 9m then move right to a grass ledge, to avoid steeper rocks above. Climb easier angled slabs then cross grass back left to the crest, which is followed to its top. Two further rock bands are surmounted en route to the summit.

The third scramble on Tarn Crag, the East Rib, lies even further to the right, reached by a slight descent.

12. East Rib, Tarn Crag

Grade 2✱ NY291072

Solid knobbly rock, exposed in places. About 80m of height is gained.

This is the continuous rock on the right end of the crags and makes the logical scrambling continuation from Tarn Crag Gill (Route 13). It is perhaps also the best continuation from Stickle Gill (Route 9).

Approach: Follow the path right under Tarn Crag, past the pinnacle near The Spur and descend slightly to the foot of the right-hand rib. From the scramble up Tarn Crag Gill cross bracken slopes to the skyline rib. Start below a steep recess which contains a holly tree. There is a cairn at the foot. See diagram, Route 11.

Route: Start up the rib which runs right of the recess. After 12m it fizzles out. Traverse left along an exposed shelf above the recess. At its end climb the knobbly slabs. Pass an overhang on the right and return to the rib, which gives fine scrambling up a succession of slabs, ribs and grooves.

Stickle Tarn is a short walk away and the scrambles on Pavey Ark and Harrison Stickle make attractive continuations.

The East Rib scramble on Tarn Crag

13. Tarn Crag Gill

Grade 2✱ NY292069

Better than it looks – the scrambling is on good rock and the interest is maintained for a considerable way. If difficulties are avoided the grade is reduced to 1. The height gained is around 150m.

This gill is an insignificant narrow stream which runs right of Tarn Crag. In the 1950s, when climbing on Tarn Crag was quite popular, this was a well-used approach route to the crag.

Approach: From the New Dungeon Ghyll car park, take the well-marked path up the side of Stickle Gill, cross the footbridge and continue to a sheepfold just over the stile. The gill is directly above; a narrow tree-lined defile on the right. See diagram, Route 7.

Route: The scrambling starts at the base of a cleft. If the water is too high the first fall needs to be bypassed. The next fall is quite difficult. Three easier steps follow to a dark recess which is passed by rocks on the right. A steep fall by bulging rocks on the left wall is climbed athletically and is easier than it looks. Regain the stream and continue up a series of steps to where the stream splits. The right branch is best, or the rocks between, to regain better scrambling in the clean streambed above. There are numerous waterslides and short steep walls to surmount. Here and there a pool traverse demands care.

A more definite ravine is met, guarded at the entrance by a square block. This ravine is mossier and contains several quite tricky pitches, an especially awkward one can be avoided on the right. Eventually the scrambling peters out.

The rocks of Tarn Crag lie to the left. Alternatively there is a small path on the left of the stream which leads to the ridge.

14. White Gill Edge

Grade 2 NY297068

A slight scramble on the spur bounding White Gill incorporates some easy rocks on Scout Crag. There is scope for climber scramblers to make a more direct ascent of Scout Crag but the route is described here in its easiest form. Rock needs to be sought to get the best out of this route otherwise it degenerates into a mainly walking expedition.

Good rock but disjointed scrambling with steep walking up bracken slopes between outcrops. The height gained is around 200m.

Approach: From the Stickle Gill car park at the New Dungeon Ghyll, start up the Stickle Gill track but almost immediately go right through a gate and cross the stream at a footbridge. Cross a tiny slate bridge, go up through a gate to a paved track. Go right through a gate and along the top edge of the intake wall, through a wood to cross the normally dry bed of White Gill. A few yards further, at the highest point of the path, ascend to the left end of the overhanging rock barrier just above. This is Middle Scout Crag.

Route: Start at the extreme left end of the lower rocks. After 6m move right onto a block and mount a rough staircase to a slabby rib on the right of a tree. The main rocks of Scout Crag lie across a stony gully on the right. Cross the gully head and descend about 15m to the foot of the climbers' descent route. This is a stony shelf on the right of a smooth rock buttress.

Climb a steep crack for 6m to the start of the shelf, which soon develops into a walk to the head of the right-hand rocks. As soon as possible, go left along ledges to reach the left edge of the rocks, which give exposed scrambling to the top of the first knoll. Climb a slabby rib on the left then go left again to the next outcrop, where a mossy slab slants diagonally right. Keep close to its edge and take care with the rock. The rough rocks in front end at a knoll, where the edge of White Gill crags is seen on the left, with a broad rock barrier across the spur above.

White Gill Edge has good scrambling in its upper part.
Photo: G.Dewitt

Reach this barrier by incorporating several tiny craglets on the way, a couple on the left then one on the right.

Right of an overhung recess in the steep wall is a slab glacis, which slants R to L. This is the route, which goes across the higher of two shelves to a grass ledge on the left. Move back right to the most continuous rock and up a groove left of a small block. Seek out the most continuous rock way to the top.

Walk above the top of White Gill then go left into a shallow combe with a low col at its top overlooking Stickle Tarn. The scrambles on Pavey Ark (Routes 16–18) or Harrison Stickle (Routes 19–22) are close by.

15. Scale Gill
Grade 1 or 2* NY303067 🌳

This shallow gill in a narrow ravine is on the southern slopes of Blea Rigg, immediately behind the FRCC Raw Head hut and the Achille Ratti hut. The gill is used for water supplies so care must be taken to avoid polluting it.

The scrambling is nowhere serious and any difficulties can be avoided. The stream is small and is a mere trickle in a dry spell. The rock is generally good. You will gain around 250m of height.

Approach: For those staying at the climbing huts, the approach is simple. Others will do better to park at the NT Stickle Gill car park near the New Dungeon Ghyll. This has the advantage of being handy for a return down the Stickle Gill path. Start by the Stickle Gill path, but leave it almost immediately to go right across a footbridge, then cross a tiny slate bridge and head up through a gate to a paved track. Branch right through a gate and go along a path above the intake wall. Cross the foot of White Gill, continue below Scout Crag and round the fell shoulder to reach Scale Gill. The path crosses the gill above a steep rocky section, which provides good scrambling and should not be missed.

Route: Descend from the path to enter the rocky watercourse. Above the path the streambed provides a mix of walking and easy scrambling. Where the ravine narrows, the scrambling becomes more continuous and awkward in places. Often there is a 'chicken run' for the more cautious on the left of the stream runnel. The final part of the gill lies up a narrow slit which is easier than it

In the narrow trench of Scale Gill

appears – apart from the final chockstone, which can be avoided just below on the right. Emerge onto the broad ridge of Blea Crag.

It is a short walk to reach Stickle Tarn and more scrambling on Pavey Ark (Routes 16–18) or Harrison Stickle (Routes 19–22).

PAVEY ARK

The cliffs of Pavey Ark, dominating Stickle Tarn, have long been a playground for rock climbers and host the most popular scramble in the Lake District – Jack's Rake.

Jack's Rake slants across the face of Pavey Ark

Pavey Ark

Easy Gully

18   16   17

16. Jack's Rake

Grade 1★★★ NY286079

An easy-angled rake, with some steeper sections, traverses fine rock scenery. The exposure of the lower cliff is hardly felt until the final stages. About 150m height is gained.

A fine way up a big cliff with no route-finding problems and little exposure until the top is neared. The rake runs diagonally across the crag and follows a trough for much of its course. The trough forms a natural drain and is often wet. On a fine day the route can be very crowded for, apart from adventurous walkers, rock climbers use it to approach or descend from the climbs. Avoid dislodging stones, particularly onto hidden climbers on the cliffs below, and be aware of those dislodged by others.

Approach: Either using the paths up Stickle Gill from the New Dungeon Ghyll or, with more interest, by the scrambles on Tarn Crag (Routes 10–12). From Stickle Tarn a path slants rightwards up scree to the foot of the rake.

Route: The first section follows a polished rocky trough below the rocks of popular rock climbs. There is a stretch of continuous scrambling either in the trough for maximum security or more elegantly on its stepped left edge,

The well-worn groove on Jack's Rake,
gives good scrambling with little exposure

Scrambling the topmost rocks of Jack's Rake, with a bird's-eye view of Stickle Tarn

to exit at a prominent tree. The rake levels briefly and passes below Gwynne's Chimney before a short steep, more exposed, step. The trough then deepens again and exits at an airy platform. Continue up the gully until the path goes left onto the front of the broad buttress. There is a well-cleaned, direct way with a steep start, but it is easiest to continue with a slight descent before the track climbs again to finish up slabs into a shallow depression with a large cairn at the top. This is just right of a prominent rock tower. Just over the wall is the walkers' path but a better finish is over the rocks on the right to the summit.

Further scrambling is found close by on Harrison Stickle (Routes 19–22).

Descent of Jack's Rake NY 288080

To find the top of Jack's Rake from the summit is not obvious. Go south-west towards Harrison Stickle, descending to a flat grass depression (cairn). There is a stone wall on the left. Just over the wall is a cairn on a slab, and another cairn is found below a rock step which marks the top of the well-trodden path of the rake.

17. Pavey Far East

Grade 2✱ NY288081

A rambling route, which finds some good rock pitches and gives close-up views of the spectacular rock climbs on Pavey's East Wall.

Approach: A path crosses Bright Beck, the north-west inlet of Stickle Tarn, and goes right of an overhanging rock outcrop, the furthest rocks on this side of Pavey Ark. See diagram, Route 16.

Route: Start on the left of the path below the left end of an overhanging outcrop a short way above the stream. Climb slabs slightly left then move right to pass the left end of the overhang. Go up a bit then climb steeper rocks above by the easiest line; **a tricky exposed pitch of rock climbing**. Climb the slabs above towards the right – there are good holds and strange circular markings in the rock.

Some interesting pitches, **difficult at the start**, some exposed sheep track, and some of the peculiar knobbly slabs that characterize Pavey. An exposed route which gains about 80m of vertical height.

Pavey Far East finishes along a roof-like ridge

This completes the first rock outcrop and the scramble seems to have fizzled out.

However, a walk left almost horizontally picks up a faint sheep track that passes below a steep little wall and the base of a slab. Continue at the same level, across two patches of bare rock above a steep drop. Go up a little and follow the narrowing bilberry ledge across more slabs to an airy descent of an exposed groove for 3m to reach a shelf round the corner. This is an excellent viewing platform especially if climbers are tackling the steep routes of the East Buttress. Zigzag up right to gain a fine knobbly slab which leads back left towards the edge overlooking Easy Gully. Climb the steep wall above on its right then walk left to the edge again. The block above is climbed rightwards by a series of shelves developing into a rib. Finally, cross a roof-like edge with hands on top and feet on the slab, to join the path at the top of Easy Gully.

To reach the foot of Jack's Rake (Route 16) descend Easy Gully, which has a short chockstone pitch.

18. Crescent Climb, Pavey Ark

Grade 4★★★ *NY285078*

This must be done as a rock climb, with belays and a sound leader. It is certainly no place for the solo scrambler and **must be done roped**; a 50m rope is recommended. There is a height gain of 80m.

This route, first ascended by Fred Botterill and W. E. Palmer in 1907, is a borderline case between scrambling and genuine rock climbing. Technically the climbing is 'moderate', which comes well within the scope of scrambling. Many of the routes described in this book have short sections that are far more difficult, but on Crescent Climb you can't walk around a section you don't like; and once embarked upon the route retreat is a serious undertaking.

The atmosphere of the route is that of a big crag – surrounded by steep rock, dripping walls and no alternative easier ways. Imagine the impression it must

have made on the pioneers, with their hemp rope and nailed boots – and no belay tapes or nuts. The rock is good on the well-marked route, but some of the flakes should be treated with caution. Several tape slings are useful.

Crescent Climb represents the upper limit of scrambling and is best done roped

Approach: Paths on either side of Stickle Tarn rise to the foot of Jack's Rake. Just below the Rake a smaller path rises left to a terrace which runs below the crags. Pass below a broad steep wall of slabs to an easier angled rib at its left end, just before the steep vegetated Stony Buttress. See diagram, Route 16.

Route *(described in pitches, with pitch length given):*

1 (42m) Follow the cleanest rocks of the rib that rises in steps. There are a few places where slings can be draped over flakes. The exposure mounts as height is gained to reach a platform. There is a flat-topped spike safe for a down-pull belay and a crack on the right which will accommodate a better nut belay. The line of the traverse below the overhangs above appears very intimidating from here.

2 (12m) Continue up the vegetated rib to the left edge of the overhangs. Slither down to a small ledge with a fine flake belay; the ledge is on the edge of an impressive void.

3 (15m) Traverse across the airy slabs below the overhangs, using comforting hand-holds and good foot-holds. The slabs stay wet after rain. It soon eases onto a grass rake. Belay at the far end.

4 (25m) Easy scrambling up slabs to a tree belay just below Jack's Rake.

Climbers taking a trip into history will take the logical continuation of **Gwynne's Chimney** (25m, 'diff'), the start of which lies a short way down Jack's Rake, just right of a rowan. This was first ascended in 1892 and is technically more difficult than the Crescent. It is steeper, more strenuous and stays greasy after wet weather. Nevertheless, it provides an entertaining route of two pitches, with more scrambling above to the summit.

HARRISON STICKLE

The bold front of Harrison Stickle must have been made with scramblers in mind for it lies at just the right angle and has just the right sort of holds and interesting rock features.

19. South-West Face, Harrison Stickle

*Grade 2** NY281072*

The lower wall on this route is a fairly serious undertaking, as it breaks through a steep band of crag. The scramble then becomes more variable and, with careful choice of route, can be prolonged up rocky ribs and walls, right to the summit plateau above.

Approach: A path on the east side of Dungeon Ghyll runs past the start, above the upper ravine. This point can be easily reached from several other scrambles or

Excellent scrambling on good rock. About 100m of height is gained.

Harrison Stickle, South-West Face

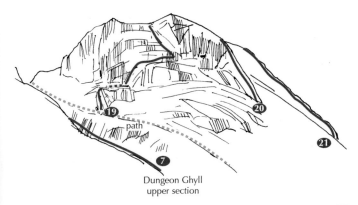

Dungeon Ghyll
upper section

71

from Stickle Tarn. The route starts where the crag almost meets the path.

Route: There is a small pinnacle just above the path at the base of a rock spur. From the grass patch behind the pinnacle, gain a slanting groove from the right. This is steep but has good holds and emerges onto a grass terrace. An easy alternative reaches the terrace by a rake on the right. Move right to the edge of the buttress and climb this on good ledgy holds, trending right to reach easier ground with grassy ledges separated by rock walls. The scramble fizzles out if you go straight up, so climb up and rightwards to pleasant rock ribs just left of the main steep buttress. Superb scrambling can be enjoyed until you suddenly emerge on the top.

20. South Central Buttress, Harrison Stickle

Grade 3✶✶ *NY283072*

A climber's scramble that passes fairly easily up steep rocks. The route offers **exposed rock-climbing situations on perfect rock. A rope is recommended.** Around 60m of height is gained.

This route accepts the challenge of the steepest buttress, which lies to the right of the preceding scramble.

Approach: From the path between Pike Howe and the upper part of Dungeon Ghyll you will see the buttress directly below the summit and to the left of a deep gully. Scramble up introductory rocks to some white slabs at the base of the buttress.

Route: Climb the subsidiary light rocks. Above is a more compact pyramid of rock, which has a light coloured base. Climb the right-hand rib of this. Where the colour changes, it steepens and is best climbed 5m left of the right end.

From the top of the pyramid a groove slants right through steep rock for 20m to a bilberry ledge (see below for direct finish from here). Ignore the tempting rocks

Harrison Stickle from Pike Howe

above which soon steepen; traverse the ledge right and it becomes a diagonally rising groove. Where it merges into steeper rock, step round a block and traverse a horizontal ledge right to easy rocks overlooking the gully. Come back left onto the slabs of the buttress front to finish satisfyingly at the mountain summit.

On the South-West Face of Harrison Stickle

Direct Finish From the bilberry ledge move slightly right then straight up on good but smaller holds. Above is another exposed passage ending below an open corner, the back of which is choked with vegetation. Take the steep right-hand edge of the corner on excellent holds to easier ground.

21. South-East Ridge, Harrison Stickle

Grade 1 NY284073

A short route, about 80m of height gain, but the rock is good.

This is a slight ridge about half way between the East Ridge and the crags overlooking the upper ravine of Dungeon Ghyll.

Approach: Easily gained from the Dungeon Ghyll path or from Stickle Tarn. See diagram, Route 20.

Harrison Stickle from Stickle Tarn

Route: There is a perched boulder on a shelf at its base. Climb a steep rock-step behind, and move left to reach a stretch of clean rock. Climb the slabs bearing left. On the crest of the spur again you can find rock almost all the way to the summit slopes. Bear right to the summit block, easiest by a groove on the right.

22. East Ridge, Harrison Stickle

Grade 1 or 2✱ NY285074

This is the stepped ridge that forms the right-hand skyline of Harrison Stickle, so prominently seen from the valley.

Approach: The lowest rocks lie just above Stickle Tarn, reached by scrambles on Stickle Gill or Tarn Crag.

Two rock tiers followed by a broad easy ridge. 120m of height is gained.

Route: The first rock tier is best avoided on the left. A terrace leads right to easy angled rocks on the ridge. Take a right trending groove to a grass terrace below a steep wall. Cross the base of this, trending right along ledges to a heather rake that zigzags to the crest of the ridge. Here easy-angled rocks rise in a series of steps. The rock is curious, completely covered in rough nodules that give an excellent grip. This pleasant section curves into a grassy rake below a steeper wall. Cross this wall, just below the highest part of the rake by a gangway that slants from right to left. A break in the gangway proves interesting. The angle eases into a walk to the summit rocks, easiest by a well-marked groove on the right, or by a more difficult direct ascent up the front at its highest point.

PIKE OF STICKLE

The profile of Pike of Stickle must be one of the most photographed views in the Lake District, with its bold rocky front extending almost 300m from its blunt summit to the screes of Stickle Breast. There are few rock climbs of any consequence on this extensive face, for the crags are rarely steep or continuous, yet its challenges to a scrambler are obvious. There are numerous possibilities ranging from the short West Ridge to a full-frontal attack. Right of the West Ridge is a longer buttress (to the left of a deep gully) and right again is the main face, guarded at two-thirds height by a steep band of grey rock. The dauntingly-steep direct approach can be avoided by traversing in from the north-west above **Traughton Beck**, which itself provides a short grade 1 scramble, or even by a scramble up Stake Gill (Route 27).

Pike of Stickle

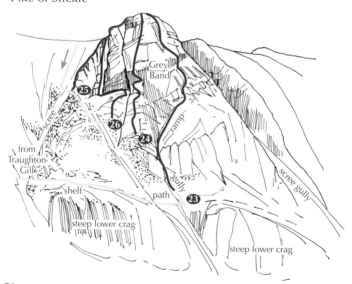

Any scramble on Pike of Stickle is an adventure for the experienced, with exposed mountaineering routes reminiscent of route finding on Alpine peaks, with the attraction of ending on a summit. In the lower part of the face there is a lot of vegetation, which diminishes as height is gained. The upper part of the mountain gives excellent exposed scrambling. **There are some poised blocks to be aware of**, although the basic rock is solid and well supplied with holds. **In wet conditions the rock becomes slippery**. To be completely safe, **scrambling here should be done roped**. Belays are not always easy to find as many of the obvious spikes are unsound and others are flat-topped. **All in all, the routes demand an experienced and competent leader**.

23. Main Face, Pike of Stickle
Grade 3✱✱✱ *NY273072*

A route which takes the easiest way up the broad frontal main face of the mountain, bypassing the Grey Band where it dwindles into insignificance at its right end. It ends satisfyingly on the mountain summit. Whilst the scrambling is not too difficult if the described route is followed, **the situation is very exposed and a rope should be used for safety in the upper section**.

Approach: From the Old Dungeon Ghyll car park, take the Mickleden path up the valley bottom until past the base of Pike of Stickle. A zigzag path mounts the steep spur on the left of Traughton Beck to emerge on a flat moor. Or you can scramble up the stream. The crags of Pike of Stickle are in profile on the right. You are aiming for a platform above the lowest rocks. From Traughton Beck the path rises to a grass shelf. Leave the main path here and follow the shelf right, where a descending sheep track leads into and crosses the steep scree gully to reach a terrace on the crag face. Continue along the terrace to a deep grassy gully where the route starts.

Initially ascends the grassy gully to break through the first band of steep, vegetated rocks (of no interest to the scrambler). Then good rock on the upper part of the peak provides excellent scrambling. **A serious mountaineering scramble, best done roped in its upper part**. About 240m of vertical height is gained. (See also introduction to this section.)

Route: Start up the gully, which proves to be slightly better than it looks. The way lies directly up the narrow rock bed, almost hidden in places by vegetation, and with the occasional steep step. Avoid a mossy wall by making a small detour right and back into the gully to enter an amphitheatre with a slabby right wall, after about 60m. Continue up the gully bed to join a sheep track that enters from the left. Follow this track up right on a broad heather slope to the foot of the main rocks at some prominent dark cracks in a steep wall. At this point the rock scrambling begins in earnest and it is wise to rope up. The steep wall is climbed at the prow, about 6m right of the cracks. Zigzag first right then left to reach a terrace at the top of the cracks. Go up left to another grass terrace. The rocks above are inviting but lead into difficult rock, so walk along the grass terrace a few feet right to a break in the wall. There is a slabby recess with an overhang. Climb the slabs and go left round the overhang to reach a groove, exit left and continue to belay at a table rock below the Grey Band.

Walk about 15m right to a point below the steep rocks, mount a perched block and the steep step above. You are now level with the top of the steep Grey Band. Continue in the same line, about 18m, along the break until just past a cleft, where it is feasible to traverse left across slabs onto the front of the buttress. Go diagonally leftwards by a line of small flakes to a ledge and leaning block.

Just right of the block, climb up a few feet to reach a line of rightward leading shelves leading across the face onto easier angled slabs and the summit.

24. The Grey Band Route, Pike of Stickle

Grade 4 and v diff✱✱ *NY273072*

This route takes the challenge of the left side of the main face, just right of the deep gully in the upper half of the crag. The Grey Band is steep and is crossed by a pitch of genuine rock climbing in an exposed situation. A rope is essential.

Approach: As for the Main Face route (Route 23) but before the starting gully of Route 23 ascend steep grass to avoid the first steep rock outcrop. See diagram, Route 23.

A serious mountaineering route with a mixture of scrambling and rock climbing with a height gain of about 150m. The Grey Band is a steep obstacle. **Only for experienced climbers/scramblers.**

On the steep Grey Band of Pike of Stickle.
Photo: G.Dewitt

Route: Start in the centre of a low rock wall directly below a prominent dark crack in the tier above. The route is described in pitches.

1 There is a shallow mossy groove with cleaner rocks on its left. Go diagonally left with a delicate exit onto a grass terrace. There is a belay 4m left of the obvious dark mossy crack.

2 Go leftwards up a break to the foot of a clean slab. Continue diagonally left onto easy ground on the right of a gully. There is a belay spike in centre of the rock wall.

3 Semi-circle right on a rock staircase to a shelf below a prominent chimney cleft formed by a huge poised block. Scramble to the foot of this and nut belay on the block on left.

4 Go round the right side of the huge block and climb a flake at its back onto a juniper ledge. Exit from the ledge at the left end, awkwardly, to reach a juniper terrace at the foot of the Grey Band. Nut belay in thin crack just on right.

5 This pitch involves rock climbing at a 'v diff' standard with no easier alternatives. Walk along the terrace for 9m to a break in the forbidding wall. Ascend bilberry ledges leftwards, then cross a rib to gain a corner on the left, which makes a steep finish. Spike belay above on right.

6 Easier ground rightwards.

7 Continue rightwards past smoother slabs to a break back left. Belay behind huge block.

8 Leftwards again to another terrace.

9 Continue to the summit.

25. West Ridge, Pike of Stickle

*Grade 3** NY273073*

Approach: By any combination of scrambles leading to the crest of the Pikes, then by-pass the summit cone by walking round the moor at its back to the Stake Pass side. You can now see a fine little ridge that starts from a grass platform 60 metres down the slope. Descend the steep slope to this platform. See diagram, Route 23.

Route: Steep little walls and ledges just right of the arête, are climbed to a steeper wall. Avoid this by a grassy trough on the right, which turns into a slab and trends back to the crest. Climb a short steep corner just right of a small pinnacle to reach a larger pinnacle. Climb the back of this by a short strenuous crack and easier rocks to a terrace below slabs defended by a steep wall. Avoid the steep wall by a diversion almost into the gully on the right, where steps on the left wall gain the slabs. Go up the arête for 6m then move right at a ledge to avoid an awkward step, thence easy slopes to join the path up the summit cone.

Quite serious, as some route-finding ability is needed to stick to the easiest route which is quite sustained. **The rocks stay greasy after rain and the exposure is considerable**. About 70m height.

26. West Gully Ribs, Pike of Stickle

Grade 2 NY273073*

Between the West Gully and the West Ridge are two rocky ribs. This scramble seeks the best combination of the two.

Approach: The route can be reached from above and is a useful filler after other routes. From the col on the Stake side of the summit rock pyramid, descend the steep slopes to cross scree to the foot of the West Ridge. Continue the descent on the spur then traverse to the base of the slabs at the start of the scramble. See diagram, Route 23.

Not so continuous as the other routes here, but the excellent rock on the upper narrow rib makes it worthwhile. Exposed in places. About 100m of height is gained.

Route: Climb the broad band of slabs on the left of the deep cut gully to a terrace. Continue up a series of grassy ledges overlooking the gully. Avoid a steeper wall by moving into the gully. At the level of a chockstone, regain the buttress front and go well left on a grass ledge below a steep wall to reach another rib left of a shallow gully. Climb the rib on its right edge (good rock) to a platform. A steep step right across the wall leads into an easier groove round the corner. Climb slabs up the rib front then move right onto a rock staircase. The narrow rib continues with interest to a narrow neck at the top of the gully, where a path is joined. Spurn the path and continue up the rocks above to the summit.

27. Stake Gill

*Grade 1 or 2*** *NY260077*

A combination of clean, rough and solid rock and interesting scrambling make this a pleasant trip. Any difficulties are easily avoided. There is 120m of height gain.

Stake Gill borders the Stake Pass path at the head of Langdale. It is well worth visiting for its own sake and can be combined with routes on Pike of Stickle (Routes 23–26). The upper part of the gill is continuously interesting. Whilst the gill is best visited when the flow is low, the width of rock makes some scrambling possible even at a medium water level.

Approach: From the car park at the Old Dungeon Ghyll, go round the back of the hotel and continue along the flat valley base of Mickleden to the head of the valley where Stake Gill is seen on the right. Leave the Stake Pass path past a clump of trees and traverse to the foot of the first waterslide.

Route: The waterslide slab makes a fine start to the route and is followed by another easier slide. The stream bends in a rock defile. Either scramble easily with the main stream or

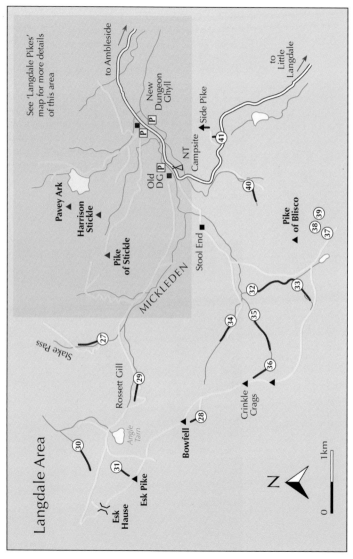

Langdale Area

See 'Langdale Pikes' map for more details of this area

to Ambleside

to Little Langdale

New Dungeon Ghyll

Side Pike

NT Campsite

Old DG

Stool End

Pavey Ark

Harrison Stickle

Pike of Stickle

Pike of Blisco

MICKLEDEN

Stake Pass

Rossett Gill

Crinkle Crags

Bowfell

Angle Tarn

Esk Pike

Esk Hause

N

0   1km

take the more difficult overflow channel to its left. The gill narrows. After a tricky start on the steep left wall, straddle the flow to reach easier ground. A more serious hazard is presented by a small waterchute around a capstone at the head of a pool. If there is too much water, escape from the gill lower down on the right. If the water is low you may still get sprayed as you pass the lip. More cascades provide good scrambling to an overhung recess. The direct route just left of the flow is possible in low water, otherwise avoid by going further left. Broad slabs continue and just when you think all is over there is another little defile to finish.

For Pike of Stickle (Routes 23–26) branch right on a small path, just as the drumlin filled hollow is entered. Or gain the head of Langstrath for the gill scramble there (Route 30).

Stake Gill has good scrambling close to the watercourse

28. Bowfell Links, Pinnacle Rib

Grade 1✳ NY245063

Above the col of Three Tarns, on the south side of Bowfell are the crags of The Links. A row of buttresses offer considerable scope for scrambling on quite good rock, but with some loose-lying blocks. The right-hand buttresses are narrow and steep in parts. Any scrambling here is verging on genuine rock climbing. In the middle, the angle is easier and the described route takes this, possibly the easiest buttress on the crag. Further left the crags become more broken and capped by a steeper tower, but the scrambling is disjointed, with many loose blocks.

Approach: The nearest parking is at the Old Dungeon Ghyll Hotel in Langdale, from where a lane leads to Stool End and the path heads up The Band. Bear left at its top to reach Three Tarns. Cross toilsome screes to the foot of the

A short, airy scramble on rough rocks; **care is required in places as there are loose blocks**. Pleasant but with a serious crag atmosphere. 70m of height is gained.

Bowfell Links from Three Tarns

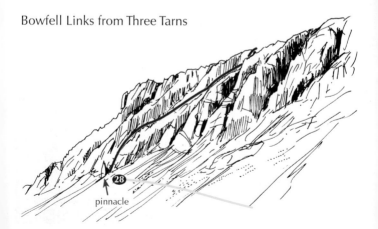

pinnacle

crags and pass below four gullies to reach a prominent pinnacle at the foot of a ridge.

Route: Climb the front of the pinnacle and move right into the gap. (It is quite tricky to ascend to the top and the descent has an awkward step.) Behind the pinnacle continue on a solid sweep of light coloured slabs interspersed with ledges.

The rock changes to grey, but is still good quality. Keep to the left edge overlooking a shallow scree gully. Where the rib merges into the gully cross to another rib on the right. This rib gives good scrambling past a steep little wall, which can be turned on the right. An easier angled rock spine emerges on a shelf with the summit ahead and the path a few yards to the right.

The rest of **Bowfell** is disappointing for scramblers – there are no worthwhile possibilities above the Climbers' Traverse towards Bowfell Buttress, although the path is very scenic as it traverses below the steep walls of Flat Crags and then ascends the screes on the side of the Great Slab. The Slab is not worth investigating, for although the angle is easy, it is mossy and slippery.

Clean rocks on the right of the path from Three Tarns to the summit provide some scrambling entertainment.

Hanging Knotts on the north side of the mountain, overlooking Angle Tarn is impressive and appears worthy of scrambling, but the rock is quite steep, despite being broken by ledges, and is very slippery in anything less than bone dry conditions.

The following scrambles (Routes 29, 30 and 31) together form an interesting excursion.

29. Rossett Slabs

Grade 1 NY252073

Approach: From the Old DG take the Mickleden track into the head of the dale. Where the path begins to rise, after it crosses the stony base of Rossett Gill, it swings left to the base of slabs.

Route: The slabs make pleasant scrambling. Where the first crag band peters out, move right onto more slabs and regain the path at the top of a knoll. The next crags are broken, so follow the path on a long zigzag left and back right to reach another continuous belt of slabs on the right. A prominent clean crag above the path is too steep for scrambling but could provide a climbing pitch.

Join the path at the head of Rossett Gill and continue to Angle Tarn.

The walk up Rossett Gill footpath, at the head of Langdale, can be enlivened by a little sport up the rocks at its side. Good rough tock.

30. Allen Crags Gill

Grade 1∗ NY243084

Although strictly speaking this belongs to Langstrath and Borrowdale it is most conveniently approached from Langdale.

Approach: At the outlet of Angle Tarn follow the path right down by the stream. The popular Esk Hause path is soon left behind as you enter the lonely head of Langstrath. Either drop down to the valley floor and take a cairned but almost imperceptible path up the side of Allen Crags Gill, or contour the steep slopes to reach the gill. The scrambling starts well up the gill, in a steep-walled straight-cut ravine.

A short but pleasant trip in a remote setting, with about 50m of height gain.

Route: The ravine is bouldery to a junction where the main stream enters from the left over slabs. Climb the rocks just left of the watercourse to a cascade in the bed of a groove with fine slabs on its left. Either zigzag easily, about 6m left of the groove, or climb the slabs direct. Continue close to the stream, up another slab into a recess where the stream splits into two channels, the left easier and less mossy. After another slab the angle eases where the ravine becomes square-cut. Climb a rib in the centre, pass a fallen block and climb a rib on the left. Pass through a narrowing in the water flow and finish up a broad rock band.

Join the main Esk Hause footpath. For a continuation scramble on Esk Pike (Route 31) at a similar grade, go left to the highest point of the path before it descends to Angle Tarn. At right angles is a broad spur which drops from the flat top of Esk Pike. This forms the route.

31. Esk Pike, North West Spur

Grade 2 in places NY240077

Good quality rough rock on a broad spur of about 60m in height. The best route needs to be sought to avoid easy ground, but some of the situations feel quite airy.

Approach: From Rossett Gill overlooking Angle Tarn, the rocks are obvious beyond the path to Ore Gap, or approach as described from Allen Crags Gill.

Route: There is a subsidiary knot of compact rock below the main slabs, about 30m right of the path. Start at the lowest left rib. Climb slabs left of a mossy streak to pass an overlap on its right. Above is a recess. Move left by 3m to ascend a steep awkward V-groove (Grade 2). Finish over a rock fin.

The main slabs lie ahead (the nearest rocks on the right). Climb these left of a mossy streak. Pass a steepening on the right and reach a grass terrace. Continue ahead up a broad, broken rib where easy ground lies just to the right. Go left to better rocks across a grassy gully. The

Esk Pike

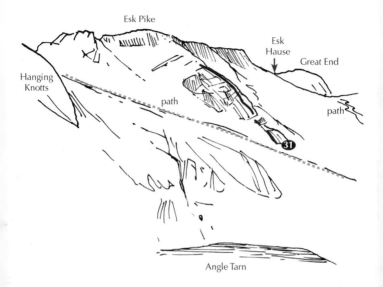

side wall of the gully is steep; step onto a sharp flake to gain a ledge. Traverse this, descending slightly to round the corner left and up a rib. Pass a bulge on the left then go back right. After easier slabs and broken ground you gain a recess, which is passed by a slab on the right of an overhang. The rib above soon curls into walking terrain and the summit ridge of Esk Pike is not far ahead.

OXENDALE

Oxendale, between Pike of Blisco and Crinkle Crags, is host to an interesting trilogy of gills, which make a fine prelude to an ascent of the higher fells.

32. Browney Gill, Lower Section

Grade 1✳ NY264051 🎋🎋

A mix of easy scrambling and walking in an enclosed ravine. The upper ravine contains less solid rock and is more serious. The lower section has a 170m height gain.

This square-cut little ravine gives a very pleasant easy scramble on clean rocks. If the water allows a passage through the first portal you should manage the rest as far as Red Tarn; in fact a trip after a little rain will add to the interest. You should be able to keep dry on the lower section. The upper gill is a more difficult proposition, with a series of fine cascades in a much narrower ravine. Escape is possible at most points. This is the best of the Oxendale gills.

Approach: From the Old Dungeon Ghyll car park at the head of Langdale continue along the road to Stool End Farm. Take the Oxendale path at the farm to the first major gill on the left; this gill cuts a deep trench from the col between Cold Pike and Pike of Blisco.

Route: The first square-cut ravine culminates in a delicate little cascade that has gouged a passage in the right wall. Ahead the character changes to a broad open stream; stick to the clean bedrock for maximum fun. At a narrowing, straddle for a few moves then transfer to the right wall and gain a ledge about 3m higher. A circular amphitheatre has an impressive exit where the stream cascades through a deep cleft. Gain the midway pool via the rib on the right, cross the lip and escape up the left wall. Grass slopes above lead to the path to Red Tarn and Pike of Blisco.

The short scrambles on Long Scar and Black Crag (Routes 37–39) are easily reached just past Red Tarn.

33. Browney Gill, Upper Section
Grade 2 or 3 ✱ 🌿🌿

If you are heading for Crinkle Crags after completing the lower section of Browney Gill, stay with the gill to scramble the upper section. Take its right fork. This is narrower and more difficult, with many cascades worth scrambling in a dry spell. Pass a huge jammed boulder on the right. At a distinctly awkward cascade where the water flows directly over a rounded rib it is time for most people to abandon the expedition and escape via the left wall. The

Difficult, wet scrambling in the upper section of Browney Gill.
Photo: G.Dewitt

upper part of the gill is only feasible in very dry conditions but gives entertaining sport for a long way. Take care as it is increasingly difficult with crumbly rock.

34. Hell Gill
Grade 1 NY260054 ♥♥

A rather forbidding ravine, due to the beetling left wall and an abundance of vegetation. The height gained is 100m.

A disappointing scramble for it is short with an unsatisfactory finish – a direct exit proves impossible. However, the scenery is impressive.

Approach: As for Browney Gill but continue up Oxendale, over a footbridge, then branch up the steep path by the side of the gill overlooking **Whorneyside Force**. (This provides entertainment for rock climbers in dry conditions when an ascent of the lower fall is feasible. The upper part is easier). Above the force, the deep cleft of Hell Gill soon comes into view on the right.

Route: Short steps and boulders are passed to an amphitheatre with a steep cascade into a deep pool. There is a red gully/chimney on the right above a scree gully. The safest exit is a horizontal path which goes out of the amphitheatre below this gully, back to the right to a rock rib. Another exit is up the scree gully and after the first rock step in the red gully/chimney take an earthy path onto the rib on the left. This has a nasty exposed step and requires care.

35. Crinkle Gill
Grade 1 *for rock scenery NY261051*

The third of Oxendale's gills is the easiest.

Crinkle Gill

Approach: From Stool End and Oxendale follow the path over the Hell Gill footbridge and into the bed of Crinkle Gill, which flows from the heart of the Crinkles.

Route: The first part of the gill lies in a narrow ravine, with one little pool which could pose a problem in high water. After a sharp left bend there is a pleasing staircase by cascades, then a long stretch of walking through a wide steep-walled gorge. At one point the best way goes under a flying buttress, where a huge rock slab has slid down the wall. The way culminates in a complex amphitheatre with a choice of four streams, the main stream being the left. Make a damp scramble up the left-hand cascade to join a path where it traverses above the stream, or avoid it by using the path which then finishes up a rock rib to the open moor.

Very easy scrambling amidst fine rock scenery. An interesting way to gain over 200m of height, but more there is more walking than scrambling.

CRINKLE CRAGS

The highest summit of Crinkle Crags is separated from the buttress of Route 36 by a long scree issuing from Mickle Door, a gap in the ridge. The buttress left of this scree is composed of steep rock bands separated by a broad diagonal rake. This rake makes an interesting scramble-walk amongst fine rock scenery.

36. Crinkle Crags Buttress

Grade 1 NY251049

Disappointing, but nevertheless it is a way up an impressive buttress of 100m to the summit ridge of the Crinkles.

This is the fine conical buttress above the finish of the gill. Despite its appearance, the route is almost entirely on grass, winding a way round rock walls by a system of easy terraces.

Approach: Crinkle Gill is the only worthwhile approach.

Route: There is a clean little stepped buttress at the lowest rocks. A grade 3 scramble can be made up this but it is

Crinkle Crags Buttress

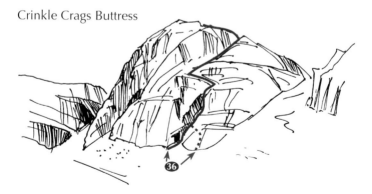

so different from the rest of the route that it is probably best avoided by using the gully on its left instead. This is right of a black streaked wall. The route is then obvious up zigzag terraces to the foot of a steep wall near the top of the crags. Go under this to the right then back left up broken rocks to the summit.

PIKE OF BLISCO

This rugged little peak has many outcrops of good quality rock, but it is difficult to string a satisfactory scramble of any length. The following short crags are worth visiting, perhaps after scrambling Browney Gill (Route 32), or more easily from the top of Wrynose Pass.

37. Long Scar, Old Holborn
Grade 2∗ NY272036

This sunny outcrop of excellent rock provides a short scramble of 14m.

Approach: Follow the Red Tarn path from the top of Wrynose Pass past a stream, and the low wall of rock is seen on the right above the path.

Route: Follow a ramp on the right wall of the central gully up cracks, then go right below a block to a ledge then follow easier rock to the top.

It is worth combining the following pleasant short (10m) scrambles on Black Crag with those on Long Scar.

This is the easiest route amongst more difficult rock climbs.

38. Little Acorn, Black Crag

Grade 3✱ NY274037

The steep outcrop of Black Crag has some popular rock climbs. The scrambles seek out the easier ways.

This takes the slabby rib right of The Needle.

Approach: From the top of Long Scar walk up and right. The crag is seen ahead and can be identified by a pinnacle, the Needle.

39. Scrambler's Corner, Black Crag

Grade 2✱ NY274037

The corner on the right of little Acorn.

More scrambling on excellent rock can be contrived. There is a low slabby wall, down on the right, which provides some sport.

✳ ✳ ✳

40. Redacre Gill

Grade 2 NY283048

Mossy, but good solid rock well endowed with positive holds. Best after a few days of dry weather when the lower fall can be climbed direct.

Little scrambling but worth incorporating, if passing, for the waterfall pitch.

Approach: The track by Redacre Gill from Wall End is the most popular walkers' route up Pike of Blisco. The ravine with the waterfall is hidden behind a spur of Kettle Crag. Traverse into the bed of the ravine from the path.

Route: Approach by scrambling mildly up the streambed to an amphitheatre of crag. The main stream cascades directly ahead. If the conditions allow, climb the fall direct to a damp mossy recess, which can also be reached by a zigzag route on the left. The upper fall is climbed on its left.

41. Side Pike, South Ridge

Grade 1 NY291052

The pert little peak of Side Pike on the south side of Langdale is a popular evening stroll, or time filler, for its ascent takes little more than half an hour and the view is panoramic. The way described adds a little adventure to the trip.

Approach: Park at the top of Blea Tarn road at a cattle-grid.

Side Pike

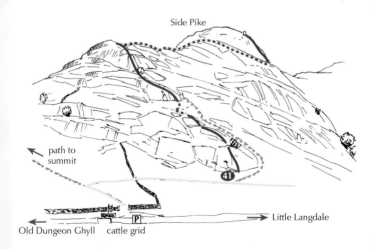

Side Pike

path to
summit

41

Little Langdale

Old Dungeon Ghyll   cattle grid

P

The South Ridge of Side Pike gives easy scrambling on good rock

Friendly rock, sound, rough and clean, gives easy scrambling with some walking between outcrops. 110m height gain.

Route: A small path branches almost immediately from the main path and traverses past a wall and below a band of rock. Climb the right end of this below and left of a small tree. Seek the best rock outcrops to reach the top of a knoll and join a path towards the summit. After a dip the path forks. Keep right, on a slightly descending path, to reach the foot of the skyline rocky ridge, which has a prominent block at its top. Climb the front of the heathery rib. At a grass ledge the easiest way lies to the right. Finish the scramble by surmounting the prominent block.

Descend by the main path along the summit ridge, to the top of the Blea Tarn road.

The best scrambling here is on the south and south-eastern facing slopes around Easedale Tarn and the following combination makes a pleasant outing of low difficulty in suitable low water conditions.

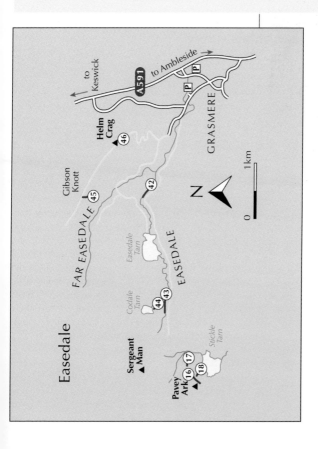

42. Sourmilk Gill

Grade 1 NY318087

A pleasant and more exciting alternative to the path with 70m height gain.

Approach: Take Easedale Road from Grasmere village. A car park on the right fills early and only local traffic is permitted past this point. There are other larger car parks in Grasmere. Go along the lane to a footbridge on the left and the path to Easedale Tarn. The path takes a level course through meadows towards the prominent cascades of Sourmilk Gill. Keep on the path as it rises until just past the last of the intake walls, then descend slightly to reach the foot of the cascades.

Route: The slabby route depends on the spread of water. Rejoin the path after a final step above a pool.

Continue on the path to Easedale Tarn, skirt the southern edge of this and continue over damp terrain towards the narrowing hillsides at the valley head. The brooding cliffs of Blea Rigg dominate the left, but on the right a fine rocky pyramid attracts the eye. This is Belles Knott, sometimes imaginatively called 'The Matterhorn of Easedale'. The main stream, Easedale Gill runs in a solid rock bed on its left, whilst a smaller but equally lively stream cascades over slabs from Codale Tarn on its right. The streams and Belles Knott are the next scrambling objectives.

43. Easedale Gill

Grade 1 NY299084

The interesting rocks of the stream are obvious as they rise suddenly from easy-angled ground, close to the path. A long glacis is topped by a short steep wall which guards access to easier angled rocks in the trough of the

Belles Knott and Easedale Gill

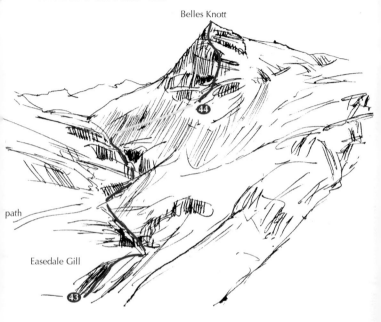

streambed. This trough winds an attractive course, always on rock, gaining 60m of height and finally exiting below Belles Knott.

44. Belles Knott

*Grade 2** NY297085*

Approach: The right-hand skyline ridge is gained from the top of Route 43.

101

Belles Knott

approach from
Easedale Gill
44

A little gem, with the attraction of culminating at a summit, although the rock pyramid proves to have a gentle grassy rear. Exposed towards the top. Avoid if damp. Height gain 60m.

Route: Start between a hawthorn and a small juniper. Climb easily between the trees, then right along a ramp to a position above the juniper. Slant left under a steep wall to a staircase of good holds and a rock terrace. Move round the right end of this and scramble up the continuous ridge, which is interesting despite easy ground on its

The top of Belles Knott with Easedale Tarn below

right in the upper part. There is a steep step above a grass platform but there are good holds just left of the arête and the angle soon eases to the summit.

Codale Tarn, a secluded spot in a rocky setting, is very close but the strata and vegetated rocks discourage a continuation scramble. A scrambling descent of the stream, which emerges from Codale Tarn, is a pleasant diversion in dry conditions. This runs over slabs to emerge in Easedale Gill close to the start of that scramble.

If a longer day's sport is required, it is not far over the ridge to Pavey Ark (Routes 16–18) and Harrison Stickle (Routes 19–22). Or, a fine return to Grasmere can be made by walking over Codale Head and the ridge which bounds Far Easedale, heading over Calf Crag, Gibson Knott and Helm Crag.

45. Gibson Knott, Horn Crag (Route 1)

Grade 3 NY317098

A scrubby crag on the side of Far Easedale holds this rather unbalanced route. (Route 2 is a more difficult rock climbing route.)

Approach: From the car park in Easedale Road, continue up the valley to a footbridge. Climb the steep hillside to the crag.

Route: Start at an easy angled buttress at the right end of the crag to reach a ledge. The steep wall above is climbed slightly right, then move left into a cleft to a ledge above. Easier scrambling leads on through the tangle of juniper (and this is almost like caving!) to the top.

A short steep rock section merits the grade and perhaps a rope, but scrambling through juniper is the abiding memory. 62m of height is gained.

46. Helm Crag

Grade 1 NY326092

Popularly known as 'The Lion and the Lamb' from the distinctive profile of its summit rocks, it is worth including in the day's outing. There are two sets of summit rocks, with a 'lamb' at either end of the summit ridge, like guardian sentinels. This is one of the few Lakeland summits to be crowned by an impressive rock ('The Lion' or 'The Howitzer', which from some angles seems more apt); indeed it overhangs on one side and forms an airy perch, reached by a short slabby scramble.

The rocky summit of Helm Crag

The descent to Grasmere is completed by a well-trodden path.

THE CONISTON FELLS

The entire eastern flank of the Coniston Fells offers much good scrambling on rock that is usually very rough in texture and is furnished with holds. There are numerous rocky outcrops that can be strung together to make an entertaining and logical progression. Whilst some of the routes are short and hardly justify a star grade individually, if combined they can provide a very satisfying scramble. The area is one of the most popular in the Lake District, yet even here the scrambler can penetrate quieter corners away from the crowds.

Do not be tempted into exploring the open holes and clefts of old mine workings in this area, for they have false floors held only by rotting timbers and the hidden chasms may descend hundreds of feet.

Car parking, transport and camping
There are car parks at Coniston, and limited free parking along the surfaced lane which runs into Coppermines Valley. Another area used for parking is at the top of the surfaced section of the Walna Scar road. Tilberthwaite has ample car parking. Coniston has bus links to Ambleside and Windermere. Campsites at Torver and Coniston.

47. The Bell
*Grade 1** SD288977*

This tiny peaklet makes a fine start to a day's scrambling. The route takes an obvious frontal rock rib.

Nice rock, good holds and 50m of fun!

Approach: Park just beyond the fell gate of the Walna Scar road. Follow the quarry road on the right. The Bell is the prominent rocky knoll on the right. After walking 200 metres along the road, at Braidy Beck, take a green path right past Bell Cottage. Keep close to a wall to cross a stream and then force a way leftwards through bracken to the foot of the rocks.

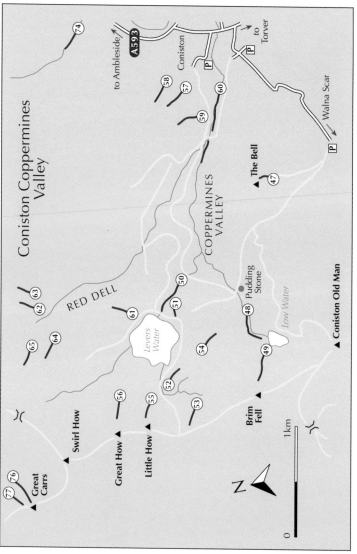

Coniston Coppermines Valley

The Bell from Walna Scar road parking

quarry road

47

Route: As you approach the rocky pyramid there is a prominent slabby ridge facing you. Start at a little flaky ridge of 9m, or a slab on the right, then move left to the slabby rocks. Follow a left slanting ramp past a juniper bush onto the front of the slabs and up to a grass terrace.

The wall above is climbed direct for 7m to a ledge. Then move right and up to a grass ledge. Escape right again to an edge. Continue directly up the ridge, or more easily just on its left. There is a horizontal terrace with a prominent tree on the right. Scramble up the back of a recess, to the left of the tree, to reach easy-angled rocks. Finally, mount rough green slabs to the summit spine.

From the top of the knoll an undulating craggy ridge leads to the quarry road close to where it turns left and heads steeply uphill. The path to the Pudding Stone and Levers Water branches right here. A logical continuation of easy scrambling is to continue up Levers Water Beck (Route 50), or a more difficult choice is Low Water Beck (Route 48) and Brim Fell Slabs (Route 49) which take you onto the fell top.

The Bell makes a good start to a day of linked scrambles

48. Low Water Beck

Grade 3★★★ SD278984

This is a popular route based on the stream which runs steeply from Low Water into the 'Pudding Stone Combe', cutting through a steep band of crags above the Pudding Stone.

Approach: Head to the Pudding Stone, either by way of the Coppermines Valley from Coniston or from the car park at the Walna Scar moor gate (taking the quarry road on the right then a traversing path from the first bend). Otherwise, you can follow The Bell scramble (see Route 47) to join the quarry road.

Route: Start at the foot of the narrow cleft from which the stream issues. A steep nose is on the right. Climb a grey rib a few feet right of the watercourse into a recess

Low Water Beck and Brim Fell

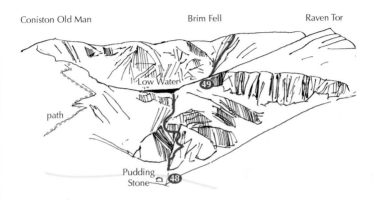

Coniston Old Man   Brim Fell   Raven Tor

Low Water

49

path

Pudding Stone

48

below a waterslide. Escape up the steep right wall on good holds, just right of a heathery corner, to a platform on top of the steep nose. The rocks above are awkwardly shelved, and become genuine rock climbing, so avoid by a diagonal rightwards ascent on a heather rake. After 20m or so, a grass ledge below a steep wall leads left onto an exposed rock foot shelf, and this is followed by heathery scrambling to a large terrace. (This pitch can be avoided by continuing up the lower rake).

A start up the beck is followed by an exposed detour on the right to regain the top of the waterfall, then excellent scrambling up easier angled water-washed rocks. A fine grey ribbon of rock is followed almost to Low Water. The height gained is 110m.

The entry pitch of Low Water Beck

The top of the waterfall is now visible and is gained by scrambling up a mixture of rock and heather, which culminates in an exhilarating leftwards stride to a recess at the edge of the stream and the end of the steeply exposed first section.

Waterworn slabs are followed to where the stream changes direction. Climb steeply on clean rock just right of the water. Ahead is a steep nose, enclosed by two arms of the stream. Ascend this by a ramp on its right. The

Low Water Beck

Pudding Stone

stream above issues from a steep barrier by an impracticable v-cleft. Climb a grassy groove 10m left then move onto the finely situated slab overlooking the stream.

The airy finish of Low Water Beck

Low Water is a short way above and the continuation scramble on Brim Fell (Route 49) makes a logical route to the fell top.

49. Brim Fell Slabs

Grade 2✶✶ *SD273983*

The face overlooking Low Water is steep, sombre and craggy. To the right, past a small stream, is a broken slabby face, which catches more sun and is composed of the typical good quality Coniston rock that makes scrambling here a pleasure.

Approach: The most interesting route is via Low Water Beck or, if there is too much water, take the quarry road up Coniston Old Man to Low Water. To reach the scramble, go round the northern side of the tarn and walk up to a small stream with a good slab on its right.

Better than it looks, on fine slabs of generally good rock, although some shattered rock is encountered near the top. **The route is quite exposed and a rope may be useful.** 190m of height is gained.

Brim Fell Slabs

Low Water

Route: Climb a broken spur that rises right from the stream then move left onto the slabs. At a grass shelf go slightly left to pick up the best rock to end the initial section. There is a short, steep wall then the upper buttress is seen as a jumble of rocks. Aim for a belt of slabs just to the right and walk below a patch of scree to the first rib on the right.

The start is quite steep but goes at the lowest right-hand point with care for some of the spikes are insecure. Easier but delightful slabs follow before an excellent

Nearing the top of Brim Fell Slabs. Photo: G.Dewitt

scramble up a more shattered buttress, ending at a steep wall. Go into the gully on its left, up this for 4m then move onto the better rocks of the gully's right wall. The summit ridge is just above.

Further scrambling on Dow Crag (Routes 79–82) can be reached by Goat's Hause, or go down the north-east spur of Brim Fell to Raven Tor (Route 54) and the scrambles around Levers Water (Routes 52–56).

COPPERMINES VALLEY

50. Levers Water Beck

Grade 1 SD283988

A rather disjointed route but the individual rock steps are quite good. The height gain is 100m.

The stream descending from Levers Water drops over several rock steps that provide an interesting way of gaining height, although the scrambling route is scrappy.

Approach: The most straightforward approach is from the Coppermines Valley using the mine track that goes past the old workings of Paddy End. The rough track crosses the stream by a bridge below Grey Crag.

If you are approaching from the Walna Scar road and The Bell scramble, take the path right from the quarry road, to the Pudding Stone (which makes an interesting ascent). Cross the stream beyond and branch down right immediately on an old track that runs below Grey Crag to the bridge over Levers Water Beck.

Route: From the bridge gain the streambed and, dependent on the water level, use the rocks as much as possible. An old incline bounds the stream on the left. The first two rock steps are most easily ascended on the left; the third is steeper and is ascended on the right of the stream. Note the old metal spikes in the streambed, this is where a mine track crossed. Start this rock step about 10m right of

the stream. Good holds trend leftwards to a ledge below smoother rocks. Move left to mount steeply, close to the water in a fine position, on comforting holds. The final hazard is a wall of crag with a waterfall at its right edge. The easiest way is by a groove on the left edge of the crag, which is ascended to a capstone. Escape right or crawl under. The dam of Levers Water lies just ahead. A more difficult alternative (Grade 3) is to traverse the left wall until near the waterfall where a steep climb is made with a move left then straight up.

Levers Water Beck

51. Simon's Nick Ridge

Grade 3✱ SD284988

From the beck the ridge looks quite short and easy-angled but turns out to be longer and better than these first appearances suggest. On the last part of the ascent of **Levers Water Beck** (route 50) there is a dark hole in the crags above to the left. This is **Simon's Nick**, a notorious feature of the region's mines. On no account enter the cleft of the Nick; **it is extremely dangerous**.

A serious route with some exposed moves high up. The rock is slippery when wet. 25m of height is gained.

115

Simon's Nick Ridge. Photo: G.Dewitt

Approach: From the top of the last fall on the beck scramble, a path leads down left and gives access to the foot of the Nick across some ochre screes.

Route: Follow the crest of the ridge, on the right of the Nick, to reach a wide platform. The rocks ahead are steep and uncompromising so move right and take an exposed line to reach a second ledge after which the exposure eases and straightforward scrambling leads to the top.

Do not be tempted to explore the open holes and clefts in this area; they have false floors which are only held by rotting timbers, and the hidden chasms may descend hundreds of feet.

52. Gill Cove Crag, North Edge
Grade 2 SD275994

Gill Cove Crag is a broad swathe of rock and vegetation overlooking Levers Water. Its north-easterly aspect ensures a liberal coating of lichen and slow drying rock. A grade 3 scramble is reported on the left-hand rib, and incorporates a nice delicate traverse, but the route described here is more in keeping with other scrambles in the area.

The rock is rather smooth, lies generally in shadow and stays slippery after rain, yet it is of good quality. **Care is required.** The scramble takes a series of rock walls along the right edge of the crags with about 80m height gained.

Approach: Either walk up the Coppermines Valley from Coniston to Levers Water, or use the shorter approach from the car parking at the fell gate of the Walna Scar track, going via the Pudding Stone and Boulder Valley. From here a path straight ahead leads to a tiny col left of Simon's Nick overlooking Levers Water. A track about 30m above the lake skirts below the crags to reach Cove Beck. The right-hand edge of the crags lies just left of the stream.

Raven Tor and Gill Cove

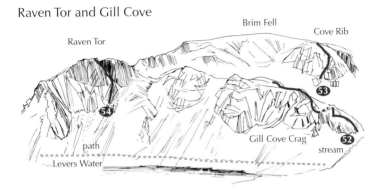

Raven Tor · Brim Fell · Cove Rib · **53** · Gill Cove Crag · **52** · stream · **54** · path · Levers Water

Route: Start at the lowest rocks left of Cove Beck; the easiest way lies about 6m up the right-hand side. After about 12m move left along grass to gain a rib by a delicate step, and mount to a large terrace. Continue straight ahead to another terrace. Go left a few metres to reach knobbly slabs just left of a rib and climb slabs to another terrace.

The next buttress drops away to the left. On its face opposite are two grass ledges below a skyline block. The first grass ledge (identified by a quartz slab) is gained by a steep ascent on good holds at its right end. Go left and climb easily to the second ledge. Slabs continue ahead – climbed first in a recess, then by a line of flakes to finish up a rib.

There are two logical continuation scrambles: across the shallow hollow of Cove Beck are the crags of Cove Rib (Route 53) whilst, if you walk further along the spur above Gill Cove Crags, the broad crags of Raven Tor (Route 54) soon come into view.

53. Cove Rib

Grade 3✱ *SD272992*

A square crag (like a castle keep with many turrets) is the most obvious feature of a line of broken crags on the Brim Fell flank of Gill Cove. The rock is slow drying due to its shady aspect, but the rock is more typical of the Coniston area than that of the Gill Cove Crags.

Approach: Either use the previous scramble (Route 52), or approach by the path heading towards Levers Hause from Levers Water until the upper combe of Gill Cove can be entered – the rocks are seen on the right.

Route: The scramble follows the left edge of the initial steep buttress then continues along a series of sharp ribs. Ascend between two small lower crags to the left

The buttress appears too steep for scrambling, but the route unfolds on good rock that is well supplied with sharp holds and pockets and finishes up a fine crest. 100m of height is gained.

Cove Rib

side of the main crag. There is a cairn at the foot of the rib. Climb easily for 8m to a steepening. Step left onto a flake and mantelshelf over the bulge onto a rock shelf – or more easily gain the same ledge by a traverse from the left. Traverse right to a grass ledge and continue diagonally right to gain a rib. After a few feet move left of the steep prong and climb steeply on good holds about 6m left of the arête. This concludes the first steep buttress.

The squat slabby rib straight ahead has a delicate mossy patch about 8m up. An easier route lies up a gully on its right, but beware of the first chockstone that appears precariously balanced. The ridge ahead is gained by a traverse across a pocketed slab from the grass gully on the left. Climb a tower on its left side. Where the ridge fizzles out, cross left to reach a parallel spur to prolong the scramble towards the ridge of Brim Fell.

The scramble on Raven Tor (Route 54) can be quickly reached by descending the spur from Brim Fell to the col at the top of the tor.

54. Raven Tor

Grade 4✶ *SD276989*

The crags of Raven Tor are easily overlooked. Although they form the northern flank of the spur above Levers Water, the crags are only fully seen from the far end of the lake. The rocks rise diagonally up the hillside, with the longest, cleanest, continuous rocks up to the right. Although there is much loose rock on the buttresses, where it is solid an army of jug-handle flakes appears to be marching up the crags. There is scope for scrappy scrambling almost anywhere, but the route described is a logical one. There is little variety, but the good rock and exposed feel of a big crag makes it worthwhile.

Raven Tor

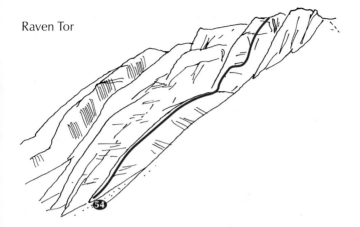

Approach: Steep screes at the side of the rocks above Levers Water lead directly to the scramble or the scramble can be approached more easily by a descent from the col at the top of the crag after scrambling either of the two preceding routes described here.

Route: The broadest buttress in the centre of the crags lies left of a red scree shoot. In its upper part the right edge of the buttress is defined by a gully. The route takes the right edge of the central buttress, first overlooking the scree shoot, then the gully. The start is marked by a small cairn a little up the screes from the lowest rocks.

The rib above the cairn gives very easy scrambling on solid flakes of rock overlooking the screes for 48m to a steeper exit onto a diagonal rake. From the topmost point of this, overlooking the gully, there is a fine sweep of steeper slabs. Climb these by the easiest zigzag route – up for 7m then left to gain a groove slanting back right to a ledge. Move right along this then continue steeply up mossier rocks about 7m left of the edge to a shelf about 40m above the rake. Easier angled, clean rocks above lead directly to the top in a further 30m.

Although the holds are excellent, **scrambling here is serious**, for the whole crag is quite large (over 120m high) and **should be regarded as a roped climb**. The rocks steepen towards the top: **do not to stray from the easiest route**. The rest of the crag has much loose rock and should be avoided.

GREAT HOW AND LITTLE HOW

From Levers Water, Great How appears as a fine rocky peak, with the lesser ridge of Little How to its left. Both provide scrambling routes away from their rock-climbing crags.

55. Little How

Grade 3 or 2✱ SD274995

The lower buttress is **quite serious and exposed** on excellent rough rock. Above, you have to search for the best rocks on a grassy spur. 180m of height is gained.

Approach: The path on the left side of Levers Water curls into Gill Cove. The path rises by the side of a stream; leave it and slant rightwards to the foot of the lowest rocks. These form a slabby spur, lower and right of a steep slab, Thunder Slab, which hosts some short but pleasant rock climbs.

Route: Start at the far right end of the broad base of the spur, at slabs rising to a quartz stringed arête. Climb the

Little How and Great How

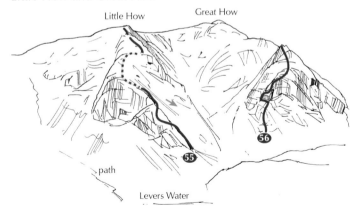

slabs then move left onto the quartz arête and follow it to a steepening. Avoid this by climbing a parallel ramp on the right and return left to the arête at the next notch. (Or climb it direct, grade 3.) The arête above the notch is still steep, so traverse left by a slab which leads nicely through a break in the steep rocks. Slabs follow to a short steep wall crossed by a groove on the right.

This ends the first and best section and it is possible to descend into the combe on the right to reach the Great How scramble (Route 56).

Scramblers on the quartz-veined rock of Little How

Little How scramble continues up the grassy spur. More sport can be found walking right, just above the level of a prominent overhanging nose, to reach a break on the right of a steep prow. A rocky rib is then scrambled to the top.

56. Great How

Grade 3★★ SD276998

An interesting route on good rock up a slabby buttress culminates in a pleasant spur to the summit. An excellent way to the tops, but **avoid in wet conditions**. Height gain is 170m.

Approach: Paths on either side of Levers Water can be used to reach the combe below the left-hand side of The Prison, the crag at the lower end of the Great How ridge. There is a ruined stone hut below a boulder slope. Keep left of this while heading up grass to the lowest rocks, a slabby spur between two screes on the left side of the crag.

Route: Easy-angled slabs rise to the foot of a steep crag with an overhung ledge at its base on the left. The ledge is awkward to gain but leads into a grassy gully. Ascend with care for about 6m then climb shelves on the right wall to reach a grass ledge below a fine slab. Walk right into the corner and ascend this to a large terrace at the top of the steep section. Above is a broad buttress with a mass

Great How

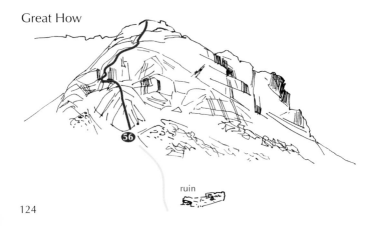

ruin

of tempting slabs and corners; it is very easy on the left, but more interesting to cross right, over some large blocks below a deep groove to a triangular recess. Climb out of the recess to a ledge on the right below a slab. Move right under this to an easier rib. Slabs and walls at an easy angle, and a small tower ascended on its left ease into walking to the summit.

Further scrambling can be reached on Dow Crag (Routes 79–82) via Goat's Hause, or on Great Carrs (Routes 76–77), which involves a descent of either Prison Band to Swirl Hause, or Broad Slack at the head of Greenburn.

CONISTON VILLAGE

The following routes are easily reached from Coniston village and provide a good start to a scrambling day.

57. Long Crag Buttress

*Grade 1*** SD299981*

Long Crag guards the entrance to the Coppermines Valley and overlooks Coniston village. The most continuous rock is a buttress at the left-hand side of the crags, which this route takes, whilst further right another sweep of rocks provides good entertainment. A feature of the rocks between is a striking columnar structure, almost like the basalt of Staffa.

Approach: Park in the village. Immediately north of the bridge in the centre of the village, a lane runs by the river towards Coppermines Valley (some parking is also available here). Shortly after the tarmac ends, go through a gate and mount the open fell to the base of the spur. The best introductory rocks lie above and left of a tree.

Superb easy-angled, rasp-rough rock and plenty of choice, with good positive holds. The rocks are well broken and almost gabbro-like in texture – a good recipe for scrambling. **Exposure mounts and novices will need to be roped**. The height gained is 160m.

Long Crag

Route: Climb the slabs, walk up the spur for 30m then move left to gain a string of mossy outcrops. Climb the slabs to the right of a small holly tree, moving right near the top to clean slabs. A steep little prow above is best avoided on its left. Continue on the crest of light coloured slabs to the foot of the steeper upper buttress. A rib curls into the steeper rocks, but the holds are excellent and the friction superb. At a grass ledge move right onto rough slabs, which run diagonally leftwards up a ramp and the rib on its right. Cross the grass gully on the right above a juniper to climb the faceted slabs above. Where the angle eases the scrambling can be prolonged by traversing right to rocks overlooking the edge of the steep right-hand wall.

The top of the crags forms the edge of a broad rocky plateau with the bulk of Wetherlam behind. To continue the day's scrambling it is best to head for a flat shelf on the left, above the entrance to the valley, where a path is picked up leading below the old quarries to contour the hillside into Red Dell. The leat below Kernel Crag can be followed to Levers Water and the wealth of scrambling around there (Routes 50–56), or Red Dell can be followed to Low Wether Crags at its head (Routes 62–65).

Topping out on Long Crag, with Coniston below. Photo: G.Dewitt

58. Long Crag, Boulder Route

Grade 2✱ SD299980

Open slabby
scrambling on
superb rough rock.
About 160m of
height is gained.

Despite some walking that splits the scramble into two sections, the rock is good and the scrambling is very pleasant. It is just a touch more difficult than Route 57. See diagram, Route 57.

Approach: As for Route 57, but just where the tarmac ends go over a stile on the right and head diagonally across the hillside to the foot of the first slabs.

Route: About 15m above an oak at the right-hand side of the slabs is a rib by the side of a gully. Mount boulders at the start of the rib, then mossy slabs diagonally left a few feet until it is possible to climb more or less direct to a flat grass platform with several square-cut boulders.

The continuation of the scramble lies well above on a buttress left of a scree gully and right of a patch of junipers. A path leads right through the boulders and across the foot of the screes to mount a parallel grassy trough. Return left to the scree gully at its narrowest point – the rocks on its left are mossy and not worth bothering with. Ascend the gully for about 40m then go left past a prominent yew to reach the more continuous clean slabs on the crest of the spur.

The slabs provide good scrambling in the centre, away from easy ground on the left. Where they fizzle out, move 7m left to another slabby rib. Pass a terrace with gnarled junipers and mount a series of steep steps in the wall above (or pass on the left more easily). A steeper tower can be turned or climbed. Ahead climb slabs on the left of a juniper then bear right to reach the final rock buttress which gives a fine finish.

59. Mouldry Bank and Rascal How
Grade 2 SD295981

An easily accessible scramble further left of Long Crag.

Approach: From Coniston gain Miners' Bridge by tracks either side of Church Beck. Mouldry Bank is the rocky spur above the road on the east side of the stream. From the bridge, mount diagonally right to the lowest rock rib below a tree.

Route: Climb the rib and pass the tree on the right. Gain a vegetated recess in the steep barrier ahead and move right to cross a bulge on good holds (avoidable left). An easy-angled rock tongue points the way past a tree to a steeper wall. Walk to the foot of the cleanest section of the final rocks and start at the lowest point. Climb 4m to

A logical line up a series of rock steps on quite good rock. 150m height is gained.

Mouldry Bank

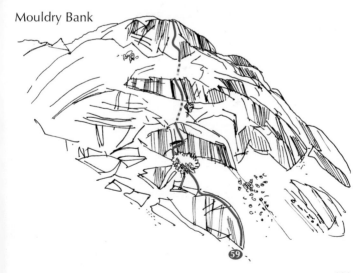

a left slanting groove. Holds are excellent. The angle now eases to the top of the knoll, where the rocks of Rascal How can be seen across a dip.

Head for the toe of an obvious buttress. The scrambling is on a thin rib with one or two tricky moves. Near the top traverse right below vegetation into an earthy gully and easy ground.

Kennel Crag lies ahead on the end of the ridge. It has an impressive pinnacle but is not suitable for scrambling. If you are heading for Upper Red Dell (Routes

Rascal How

If you want to see some of the remains of the area's mining history return to the dip between the two sections of the scramble, where a path right soon joins a quarry track descending to the main path up the eastern side of the Coppermines Valley above Irish Row.

At the top of Red Dell waterslide note the abundant evidence of old mining activity. Above and right of the old masonry tower is the old engine shaft of Bonsor Mine. If you have a torch it is worth going just into the tunnel to the edge overlooking the balance bob platform. Across this is the 423m deep shaft! For further information about the mines in the Coniston area see *Coniston Copper Mines – A Field Guide* by Eric Holland (Cicerone Press).

62–65) continue directly up the valley bottom; if you are going towards Levers Water cross the col directly below Kennel Crag to join a horizontal track which joins the pony track to Levers Water (Routes 52–56). Going this way, the scrambler can continue along a little used pony track towards Levers Water Beck (Route 50) and incorporate the best bit of that route.

60. Church Beck, Coniston

Lower Section Grade 1∗,
Upper Section Grade 2∗ SD297977

A surprisingly good trip with a striking ravine, several waterfalls and deep pools, some of which are popular bathing spots for village children.

Approach: Go up a lane to the left of the Sun Hotel (the start of the Walna Scar road) and the path that follows, signed 'YH'. Go through a meadow and where the rough lane rises steeply gain Church Beck at a bridge on the right.

Route: The first cascade is soon reached, the rock bed fretted and scoured into attractive shapes. Reach a weir

Church Beck usually carries a lot of water yet gives a popular scramble if you are prepared for some wading. The rocks are smooth and slippery. The height gain is 90m.

in a sylvan setting. Gain the central rib and go left up the dry riverbed. The walls converge into a gorge, which you enter by wading through shallow water on the left-hand side. Pass into this impressive defile and climb slabs by the side of a cascade. Cross to the right to bypass a pool. Another waterfall is climbed on its left to reach yet another fall, which is unfortunately impassable as it is situated between steep walls with a deep pool at its base. Return to the lip of the previous fall and escape right (facing downstream). A slight path in the bracken joins the lane above to end the first section. Regain the stream by a ledge just below Miners' Bridge. On the left is an old mine level which can be explored if you have a torch. It begins with a wade. See *Coniston Copper Mines – A Field Guide* by Eric Holland (Cicerone Press).

On Church Beck, the fall below Miners' Bridge can be climbed at grade 3

The rocks of the fall can be bypassed, or climbed at a much higher grade than the rest of the trip. Wade to the central rib, climb up to the right side of a prow and

ascend the vertical right wall of this on widely spaced
holds, good at the top (grade 3). If the water allows, an
easier ascent may be made bearing left at the top. Pass
under the bridge to another small ravine. Where it twists
to reveal a cascade exit on a ramp on the right. Regain
the bed and round the corner is a final cascade, which is
easily climbed.

The flat floor of the Coppermines Valley lies ahead,
with access to numerous scrambles.

61. Sunlight Slabs

Grade 2 SD282994

On the right-hand (east) side of Levers Water is a tumble
of ribs and slabs. This short slight scramble takes more or
less the prominent rib, although other ways can be found.

Approach: Either walk up the Coppermines Valley from
Coniston (or incorporate Route 60) to Levers Water, or
use the approach from the car parking at the fell gate of
the Walna Scar track, going via the Pudding Stone and
possibly Route 50.

Route: Start at the foot of a prominent long rib. Avoid the
first steep section by the gully on its right then ascend the
arête with an excursion onto the easier ground on the
right. From a terrace the rib is climbed on its left side.

This leads to the ridge above Red Dell. The scramble
on High Wether Crag (Route 65) can be reached by
ascending the ridge for about half a mile to a flat area
high on the ridge just below a rocky step. The terrace
right leads below the crags to the scramble.

Good rock but the
best route involves
using small holds
and rock-climbing
situations. Disjointed
if easier ways
are sought. 50m
height gain.

RED DELL

Whilst the scrambling possibilities of the ravine and waterslide slabs above the mine building look enticing, the ravine has an impassable fall and the waterslide slabs are coated with a broad veneer of slippery gunge. It is better to walk up the path to the following routes in Upper Red Dell!

UPPER RED DELL

The upper part of Red Dell is one of the least visited corners of the Coniston Fells; the path up the valley is slight and the valley head is a wall of crag, especially on the left.

Approach: Just above Miners' Bridge over Church Beck a track forks right. This rises past the ruins of Bonsor Mine into the valley of Red Dell. The first vegetated crag, Erin Crag, is unfit for scrambling. Low Wether Crag and High Wether Crags invite attention. Well above the sheepfold, on the hillside right of the stream is the compact knot of Lower Hows.

Upper Red Dell

62. Lower Hows

Grade 2✱ NY286003

Route: Start at the lowest point of a broad slabby base, where there is a cairn. Go directly up for 20m then left below the overhang to easier ground. Continue to a shelf. Ascend rocks about 3m left of a fine arête and follow the easiest route to a terrace. A crack splits an overhang. Climb to the base of the crack then avoid it by the slab on the right. The angle eases but slabs give good scrambling well up the hillside.

The best type of Coniston rock with slabs the texture of gabbro. This is a good way to the top of the Lad Stones Ridge of Wetherlam. 80m height is gained.

63. Upper Hows

Grade 2 NY287004

Descending slightly from the top of the main rocks of the previous scramble, across the hillside to the right is another crag, which is steep in its lower part. This route gains about 60m of height.

Only worthwhile as a continuation of Route 62 in order to seek more rock on the way to the fell top.

Route: There is a messy gully just left of the lowest rocks which can be used to gain 6m or so, after which traverse rightwards to gain clean, easy ground. Rocks are followed pleasantly until they peter out not far from the Wetherlam ridge footpath.

Several hundred yards down the valley to the right of Lower Hows (NY 288001) is another three-tier succession of craglets, which give a mild scramble.

64. Low Wether Crag

Grade 3✳ NY284002

Good rough rock, but the upper part of the scramble winds onto the greasier north-facing side, which needs a few days dry weather. Belays are not easy to find. **A serious route, rope advised**. 70m of height is gained.

This is the third major outcrop up Red Dell, the first being Kernel Crag and the second Erin Crag.

Approach: Either strike a diagonal line up the steep hillside just after passing a sheepfold, or walk until opposite Lower Hows and mount steeply to the right-hand side of Low Wether Crag.

Route: Take a line up the easier-angled triangular buttress at the extreme right of the crag. Start at the bottom of the light coloured slabs just to the left of a grassy break. Ignore the cairn below the slabby rib on the left, which marks the start of a rock climb ('diff'). Climb the slabs using small positive holds to a large grass ledge. Above are more slabs, less compact than the lower ones, to another grass ledge. The buttress is narrower and more broken here and the best way on is up steep grass to the left, beneath the impending wall of the adjoining crags.

Continue over broken rocks and bilberry patches to arrive at the bottom of a steep ridge which borders a grassy chimney to its right. Climb the ridge, which

Low Wether Crag

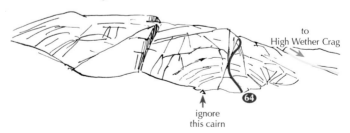

to
High Wether Crag

64

ignore
this cairn

is awkward and exposed at first – the rock can be greasy until easier-angled, cleaner rocks are reached. Scramble over these and the quartz-veined blocks to the top of the crag.

Walking northward, the next rocks are at the lower southern end of High Wether Crag. A terrace runs to the right below rocks composed of superb bubbly rock set an ideal angle for scrambling. There are numerous possible scrambles, which gain in height as one moves right. At the end of the crag is Route 65.

65. High Wether Crag
Grade 2∗ NY284006

This is above a grass terrace, high on the left side of upper Red Dell. The rock here is very good and the longest scramble lies at its right end.

An airy, exposed scramble on good rock easing after a steep start. 80m of height is gained.

Approach: Either by Route 64 or a very steep ascent from the upper Red Dell valley floor or more easily from the ridge (easily gained from Levers Water) where a flat terrace below a rock barrier leads right below the crags. Start at the right-hand end. See diagram, Route 62.

Route: Start below a rock rib, with a small pedestal at its foot, just left of the right-hand end of the crags. There is a cairn here. Climb the prow for 9m to a bilberry ledge. Go diagonally left then back right across a grass ledge to easier angled rocks. Good scrambling straight ahead, passing two grass ledges. After about 30m, move right for 9m, below a steepening, to a rib which fizzles out in grassy slopes.

The summit of Wetherlam is a short walk away.

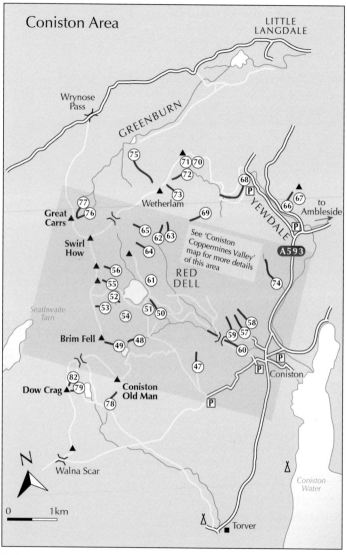

Coniston Area

LITTLE
LANGDALE

Wrynose
Pass

GREENBURN

75

71 70
72

73
Wetherlam

68
P

67

66
P

to
Ambleside

69

77
76

Great
Carrs

65

62 63

64

See 'Coniston
Coppermines Valley'
map for more details
of this area

A593

Swirl
How

56
55

61

RED
DELL

74

52
53

54

51 50

58
57

Seathwaite
Tarn

Brim Fell

49 48

59
60

P

P
Coniston

47

82
79

P

Dow Crag

78

Coniston
Old Man

N

Walna Scar

0   1km

Coniston
Water

Torver

YEWDALE AND TILBERTHWAITE

Yewdale cuts into the fells to the north of Coniston. Narrow lanes lead up either side of the stream, the one on the left to a popular car parking area at Tilberthwaite Quarries. The right-hand lane goes to Hodge Close Quarries, an interesting deep hole with a flooded base, popular with divers and rock climbers. Raven Crag near the valley entrance has an excellent scramble, and Wetherlam offers further sport.

66. Raven Crag, Yewdale

*Grade 2*** NY311002*

Although Raven Crag has access restriction due to nesting birds (between 1 March and 30 June), this usually applies to the climbers' steep flank of the crags, whereas the scramble takes the easy-angled broad buttress front. Check the BMC or FRCC websites for latest information.

The rocky spur of Raven Crag, Yewdale, with the shorter spur of Pussie's Paradise behind

Raven Crag, Yewdale

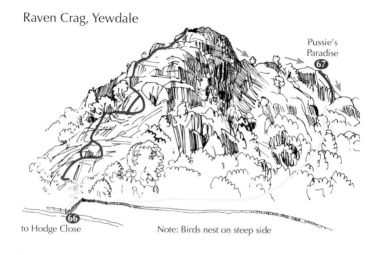

Pussie's
Paradise
67

to Hodge Close **66**

Note: Birds nest on steep side

Entertaining scrambling on sound rough rock, seeking the best way and not too serious: a good introduction to the sport. **Novices may need a rope in places**. 130m of height is gained.

This fine rocky buttress is easily seen from the Coniston–Langdale road.

Approach: Park along the narrow lane on the north side of Yewdale (signed Hodge Close), either almost immediately just before the bridge or further along the narrow lane, before or after the access point. Remember the lay-bys are also passing places. The rocks almost meet the road and there is a stile over the fence at its junction with a wall. Cross this and take a path which goes directly up, by a wall to a gully in the first crags.

Route: Descend to climb pleasant slabs left of the gully, then either continue through bracken or go right below the steep wall at the top of the gully to gain easier rocks. Either way leads to a grass terrace with a pyramid of grey rock at its left end. Climb the pyramid either by a groove on the right, or the slab on its left flank. Move right again to further rocks rising in steps to a steeper section. Continue by a mossy groove ahead or, for a more elegant line, go

Raven Crag, Yewdale, has a succession of interesting rock steps

diagonally right past a black mossy streak to a sloping platform on the edge. Now climb a slanting rake bearing left below steep rocks. Go up the rake, climb a short steep rock then easy-angled rocks slanting left to reach a fine tower. Climb this directly by a system of rock ledges. The steepest part is now over but climb easy rocks towards a prominent tooth dominating the skyline. Just below this is a steep wall, climbed by a break right of centre. This leads to a little stepped rib up the prominent tooth.

A direct descent is unpleasant due to dense bracken so it is best to walk over the heathery rocky knolls of the fell top to Uskdale Gap where paths descend on either side for a return to the car. Alternatively, you could include the following short scramble (Route 67) on the way.

67. Pussie's Paradise
Grade 2 NY313003*

Short but interesting on good rock. Belays are scarce for roped ascents. There is a 45m height gain.

Approach: From the top of the Raven Crag scramble (Route 66), at about the same level but to the right at the head of a slight combe, you will see a crag of clean rock. Though it is visible from the cairn at the top of Raven Crag, direct access is barred by dense bracken. It is best to go along the ridge, past a decrepit wall and a gap, then over small knolls to the prominent clean rock knoll which tops the Pussie's Paradise ridge. Drop into the shallow dip beyond and turn down this to the foot of the scramble, which is marked by a pinnacle with a wall of fluted rock above. See diagram, Route 66.

Route: Start on the left side of the pinnacle, move up the base of the flutes, then up a heathery wall on the left to a platform. Move right onto the rib, avoiding a dangerous perched block. Continue above the block on a gangway leftwards to a grass shelf. Climb a ridge to another shelf.

There is a heathery wall on the left and an easy outcrop to finish.

A steep, slight path descends to the road from the foot of the scramble but it is preferable to continue a walk along the fell top as described after Route 66.

Pussie's Paradise has a difficult start, which can be avoided on the left

143

68. Tilberthwaite Gill

Grade 2 on the entry pitch✱ NY304006

A steep walled ravine, narrow and awkward of entry becomes broad and easy to a narrower exit.

A rather disappointing scramble lacking in continuous interest, but it does provide a scenic approach to Wetherlam. In Victorian times there was a constructed walkway and bridges to view the delights; now there is a single viewpoint bridge (which goes nowhere) spanning the lower part of the ravine.

Approach: The lane up the left side of Yewdale leads to parking below quarry spoil at the foot of the gill. Take the path up the left side of the gill and fork right to go down to a footbridge. Follow the gill to an abrupt bend where the gorge begins. 90m is gained in height.

The Gill Head finish of Tilberthwaite Gill.
Photo: B.Freed

Route: The description is based on normal low water conditions. In wet weather the stream carries a large volume of water when the ascent of the first part would be quite terrifying. The first pool can be traversed on the right (awkward if water level is up) then walk under the footbridge to be faced with a tricky obstacle. Scramble up sloping ledges on the left wall to avoid the waterfall (this is exposed and rather slippery). There are no further difficulties to the confluence of streams. Either scramble out by the left branch or take the right branch to Gill Head Waterfall which has a mine level at its foot. After a look in the mine entrance most scramblers will retreat to escape at a convenient break. Rock climbers can make a very difficult and slippery exit by a pitch on the left of the fall.

At the head of the gill join the main path on the right towards Wetherlam. This leads round the edge of a broad flat basin, Dry Cove, where further scrambling can be followed.

69. Swallow Scar

Grade 2✱ *NY294002*

Approach: On the eastern side of Wetherlam is a deep combe with the prominent dark crag of Hen Tor. The left end of the combe is the spur of Steel Edge, which has a path starting from the entrance to the broad, flat basin of Dry Cove. Follow the path up the spur to the foot of rocks, then branch left under the crags to reach a more continuous belt of clean rough slabs. **Note that a direct ascent of the vegetated crags below the clean upper slabs is not recommended.**

Route: Start at the toe of a rocky rib where the path goes over small boulders just past reddish scree. Scramble up the rib, keeping to the cleanest rocks.

Good but short. 70m of height is gained.

BIRK FELL

This is the subsidiary shoulder traversed by the Wetherlam path at the head of the flat basins of Dry Cove. There are several short crags of ideal clean scrambling rock above the old workings of Borlase Mine.

70. Route One, Borlase Crags
Grade 1✱ NY297016

Pleasant scrambling on clean, easy-angled rocks in a beautiful area which catches the sun. **Care needed with some loose flakes.** 70m of height is gained.

Approach: Follow the miners' track from the top of Tilberthwaite Gill round the hollow of Dry Cove Moss to the spoils of Borlase Mine amongst some isolated pines. Note numerous stumps of old trees in this area. The route starts where the path steepens at ruins of miners' buildings.

Route: Just above the ruins are several short pale-coloured outcrops. Start at the first one, which is shaped like an inverted triangle. Start at the toe of the first buttress and climb it. Walk left and cross shelving rock to the edge. Emerge at a level area with trees. The path arrives at this point and after following it through a gap in the wall,

Birk Fell

walk left to the lowest point of the next outcrop, longer and steeper than the preceding ones. Climb the rib, steep at first. Move left again and pick up the next rib to the top of the outcrop. The path comes close to your route again, so move left for the best scrambling to the fell top.

71. Route Two, Borlase Crags

Grade 3* NY295017

This is on the steeper buttress up to the left of Route 70, from which it is easily gained.

Route: There is a rocky shelf at the base of the crag and the route starts near its mid point. Climb easy stepped rocks for 4m into a grassy bay then move left, passing a small juniper bush. Continue up and left to reach the left edge of the front face. Move up to gain a sloping ledge below a short steep wall. This wall can be climbed direct but the moves are tricky and not easy to protect. Alternatively an insecure traverse rightwards across the narrowing ledge (care with rock) leads to a break in the wall. Climb this to a broad rocky terrace. The crux is now over. A rib provides a continuation. When it peters out, move left across the top of a small gully to climb onto the rightmost rocks of an adjacent buttress.

Quite serious with exposed situations. **Rope advised**. 40m of height gain.

WETHERLAM

72. Glassy Crag

Grade 2 NY293013

This is the broad area of crag, well to the right of and lower than Hen Tor, which is the prominent steep buttress

Slippery when wet. 150m of height is gained.

Glassy Crag, Wetherlam

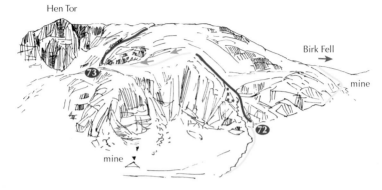

Hen Tor

Birk Fell

mine

73

72

mine

under the summit of Wetherlam. The crags stretch around the flat boggy basin of Dry Cove to the left and at a lower level than Borlase Crags. There is a lot of rock hereabouts, but it is hard to compose a scramble that is not too difficult. This is one solution, but is rather disjointed with some steep grass.

Approach: Either descend steep slopes from the col at the left end of Birk Fell after Routes 70–71, or make a direct approach from the boggy hollow. An old mine working on the edge of the hollow has a tiny stream on its right. Follow this to where it emerges from the crag at its lowest point.

Route: Climb rocks on the immediate right of the stream then walk up grass towards a steep wall. The front of the slab to the left of the stream can be climbed at a higher standard or bypassed on its right. A slender rock rib on the left of the stream, with a short steep right wall, leads well up the hillside. It is best abandoned at a small notch where a sheep track crosses. Follow this left to reach Route 73.

73. Glassy Crag Continuation Ribs
Grade 2 NY292010

Approach: Cross the hillside leftwards from the top of Route 72 to reach a grass shelf well before Hen Tor. Above the shelf are several areas of rock; look for a clean rock rib, about the third one from the left end of the crag.

Route: Climb the rib by its right edge using good holds. Reach a flatter, grassy area. Above is a wide grassy gully with a stepped rocky ridge running up its right flank and more broken crags on its left. Climb the right-hand ridge on its steep left edge. The rocks above lie back and continue until petering out near the top of the fell.

Pleasant scrambling, with big spiky, sometimes loose holds on the lower section. The upper part has some steep sections on less juggy, but rougher and sounder rock. 150m of height is gained.

✳ ✳ ✳

74. White Gill
Grade 2 or 3 SD297989 🌲🌲

The steep craggy hillside of Yewdale Fells borders the Coniston–Ambleside road. White Gill is the waterslide that spills down the fellside.

Approach: A path runs through the woods, parallel to the road, from Coniston to the entrance of Yewdale and crosses the stream.

Route: Choose the driest way up the slabs.

Water-washed rocks, which are most often black and wet across most of their breadth, give **slippery and exposed balance scrambling. Take care**. 120m of height is gained.

This offshoot of Little Langdale cuts into the fells on the north side of Wetherlam. The easiest access is from Fell Foot Bridge in Little Langdale where there is limited parking. Better parking is available further up the road.

75. Long Crag, Wetherlam

Grade 1 or 2✱ NY284017

This lies on the Greenburn face of Wetherlam, a long route in a secluded situation. A succession of craglets mount a long spur. Where this merges into the hillside the route takes the right side of the broken crag to the left. It is an interesting, unusual way up Wetherlam, with fine views.

Approach: From Fell Foot Bridge take the track past Bridge End to join the old mine track up the valley. At the

Long Crag, Wetherlam

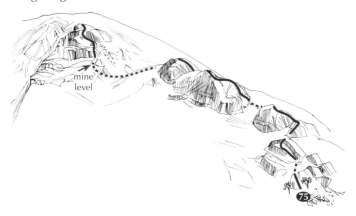

Long Crag, Top Section

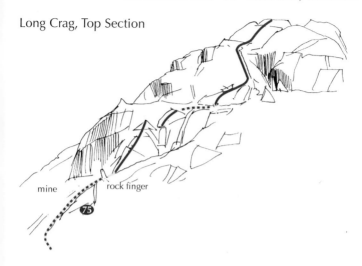

mine   rock finger

75

mines the driest route takes the right fork, to keep close to the stream. Cross the embankment of the usually dry lake. The scramble starts straight ahead up a craggy spur.

Route: Start at the foot of the spur directly above the tarn, at a nose of rock between two trees. There is a cairn here. Climb the steep nose and easy-angled slabs. Go slightly right to a smooth green scoop. Move left below a steep block to climb the left edge of a short chockstone chimney, then through boulders and up slabs and a crest to the top of the first knoll.

Ahead is the next craglet, too steep at its left end, but with a right slanting ridge below. Follow the ridge and near its top climb the clean nose on the left. The next craglet lies across a gully and has some interesting rock. There is a prominent knife-edge rib gained by crossing the grass gully. Reach the edge from a ledge on its right and climb the ridge. Move left across a gully onto clean slabs to the top of a pointed rock. (Another way gains this point more directly by a shallow groove.) Stride boldly

A long scramble, it is about 300m in vertical height, disjointed in parts and open to much variation. The rock is rough and solid, clean where it catches the afternoon sun, but green and slow drying in the shade.

across the gap. Go straight ahead up grass and boulders then up a groove, steep to start, in a slabby outcrop. Move horizontally left to easy-angled slabs of perfect rock with many options, to the top of the long spur. Ahead scree slopes rise to the summit plateau, but on the left is a jumble of steep crag, which hosts the top section of the scramble.

Take care to locate the correct route; if you stray too far left you will find the rock is more vegetated and greasy. Walk left across two scree spoil heaps. Just past these another small scree comes from a gully. Look up to locate a small drystone wall, with a mine trial level hidden above. The scramble restarts on the rock rib to its left. Climb the rib, first left then right, then straight ahead. On the left is a bilberry groove; climb this by its left slabby side then go up grass to a moss-speckled slab. Climb the centre of this to a ledge with a large boulder. Escape right onto a long easy rib to a grass ledge up left. Go back right up a short slanting crack and follow further slabby rocks to the top.

Wetherlam's summit stands a short walk above. Other scrambles on the Greenburn face of Great Carrs (Routes 76–77) are easily reached from Swirl Hause, the col between Wetherlam and Swirl How.

GREAT CARRS

At the head of Greenburn, Great Carrs presents an easy-angled, rocky face, with plenty of grass interlinking and surrounding the outcrops. Although the rocks are discontinuous, they are ideally suited to scrambling, for they are clean, rough and sound. One can scramble anywhere and avoid difficulties at will, but the diligent seeker of rock can link slabs, walls and spiky arêtes to make a lengthy, enjoyable route which ends almost on the summit.

76. Great Carrs Buttress

*Grade 2** NY274012*

Approach: The shortest approach is from the top of Wrynose Pass, but the longer walk up Greenburn (park at the base of Wrynose Pass above Fell Foot) past the mines is quite interesting. Indeed at the mines the stream has been diverted into a short narrow ravine, which makes an interesting short ascent. Once past the old reservoir continue up grassy slopes to the lowest crags. Either scramble up these or take the grass slopes on the left until a first steep knoll capped by a prominent perched block is seen. The scramble proper begins under this.

Alternatively, as part of a longer mountain day, the rocks can be approached by a traverse of the hillside from

Pleasant scrambling despite a short walk in the middle. 230m of height is gained.

Great Carrs from Greenburn

Swirl Hause. The line of the route, and the perched block, is more obvious from this side.

Route: Start at the left side of a rib at a blunt nose capped by a perched boulder. Scramble up a grass ledge to the left of the steep nose, then a rock groove gives access to slabs and the perched block. The ridge now rises in short steps. The route can be varied to include the most continuous rock, which offer very good scrambling, first to the right then back left until it eases into walking. The summit crags come into view. The most continuous rib is reached by crossing scree on the right. Do not go too far into the gully. The route develops into a spiky ridge with good holds, which despite its appearance, proves quite easy and runs into the broadening slopes of the gully. For a good finish, move across to the next rib on the right which is steep and interesting.

77. Great Carrs, Central Buttress

Grade 2✱ NY273011

Some good situations. 230m of height is gained.

Approach: as for Route 76.

Route: Walk up the shallow gully in the centre of the crags until the first real rocks are encountered at a steep little wall on the right. Ascend the nose and clean rocks above, which develop into a buttress of walls and ledges – on one of these a large flake leans against the wall. Climb this by its left flank and step on the wall above, to a large grass terrace. Go any way up small walls, as it becomes more vegetated, to a scree patch under a steep wall. Walk up the grass rake on the left to gain rocks which run up to the left skyline of a rock pyramid, climbed steeply on good holds. There is grass above this to broken walls and ribs. Then cross a steep section via rocks close to a gully. On the right is a fine spiky rib.

Walk to this and climb it, first on the right then crossing to the left at about halfway. There is easier scrambling along the crest to the top. If this rib is thought too steep, easier rocks to the right can be ascended.

✳ ✳ ✳

78. Coniston Old Man, Goat Crag

Grade 1 SD268973

This easy scramble up a fellside littered with small craglets provides an unusual route up the Old Man. The craglets follow in rapid succession with little walking between, and can be varied at will. This is a scrambling, bouldering and walking route.

Approach: Park just inside the fell gate at the start of the rough road to Walna Scar. Before Torver Beck take the path right towards Goat's Water. Where the path levels the craggy hillside can be seen ahead just above the path. Pass mine spoils, and 400m past a white cairn the path turns left below the jumble of rocks. Start just past a small stream where boulders reach the path.

Route: Start at the second of two small outcrops, which is a short, pocketed slab. Walk left to larger slabs (there is a cairn below the left end). Climb either side of a recess (the right side is more difficult). Go straight up the easy-angled slab above. Climb a steep, flaky wall at the right end of the next outcrop. A rib leads into a deep groove in the block above. Ascend a slabby rib on the left then go diagonally left to the bottom of a steep face. Go left along a rock ledge to easy spiky rocks. Just above, an outcrop is climbed by a smooth groove to emerge on the right.

Climb the spiky ridge ahead onto the pyramid-shaped rock that is so noticeable from the base. Where the ridge levels out to merge into the fellside go left below

The knobbly rock here gives a firm footing even when damp. Flake handholds are found in abundance but their tops are thin and friable – take care. The route is not at all serious but the 200m of height is gained with interest.

Coniston Old Man, Goat Crag

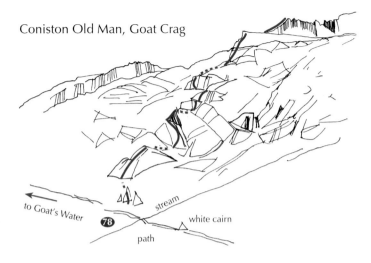

to Goat's Water

78

path

stream

white cairn

crags. Climb the edge by a shattered rib. Broken rocks continue for a considerable way up the fellside; go leftwards for the best route that includes a short chimney with earthy foot-holds, a corner crack, a face and a crack with a difficult start. Above this the rocks fizzle out onto the summit slopes of the Old Man.

DOW CRAG

The magnet which draws climbers to the Coniston area is the impressive array of crag giving its name to the peak overlooking Goat's Water. Many of the climbs are very popular, resulting in polished holds and little trace of grass or loose rock. Away from the popular climbs, on scrambling terrain, the opposite applies – there is an abundance of grass, loose flakes are common and the nature of the rock defeats all attempts to find a good quality scramble without considerable recourse to grass or including some steep rock moves. Thus any scrambling on Dow is serious and can only be recommended to those with rock-climbing experience and route-finding ability. A rope should be used to protect the most exposed passages.

The buttresses are named alphabetically from left to right. There is a prominent blue rescue box at the foot of B-Buttress.

Approach: The most popular approach is to park along the Walna Scar road past the fell gate. Follow the rough track until just before Torver Beck; at a large cairn a path up to the right takes you into the combe and to Goat's Water. Either climb a zigzag path directly up screes to the foot of Easy Terrace, or take a more circuitous way to the blue rescue box at the foot of B-Buttress where a horizontal path under the crags is found.

Alternatively, Dow can be incorporated into a scrambling day on the Coniston Fells. From Goat's Hause, at the head of the combe, a slight but improving track traverses the scree to the foot of the buttresses.

Dow Crag from Goat's Water

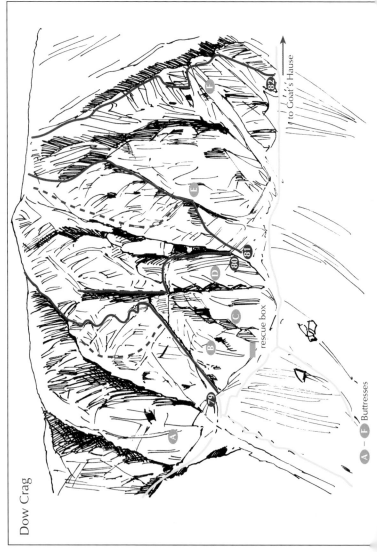

Dow Crag

to Goat's Hause

rescue box

A – F Buttresses

79. Easy Terrace and its continuation
Grade 3✳✳✳ SD263976

This incorporates the climbers' descent from a terrace above the steep lower section of B-Buttress and continues up broken rocks of the upper section, with some steep steps, to the top. The upper buttress has been well trodden by scramblers into a logical route and is easier than the original way via the climbers' descent from the

This is the most used of the scrambles on Dow and thus the rock is fairly good. **The upper part is exposed and quite serious as belays are difficult to find.** Once on the route there is no escape. Beware of stones being dislodged by climbers coming down their descent route. 130m of height is gained.

Easy Terrace starts up a broken gully

159

top of B-Buttress's upper section. The route traverses some fine rock scenery. **Taking a rope and helmet is advised**.

Approach: From the Rescue Box under B-Buttress, follow a track left under the crag into the deep recess of Great Gully where a ramp slants diagonally up to the right.

Route: Gain the base of the gully ramp from the left. Climb the gully and the cleaner rocks on its right until forced into the gully. This narrows to a squirmy greasy exit, or preferably it can be avoided lower down by moving onto the right-hand rib again. Well-trodden easier scrambling leads to where the path levels (see box below for alternative finish). Do not continue on this as it goes to the top of the rock climbs; instead climb the slabby gangway overlooking it. This mounts to an exposed perch overlooking a gully. The route now climbs the buttress above in a series of zigzags up walls and ledges starting with an exposed traverse left. The way is very well worn but the mounting exposure justifies the grade and belays are difficult to find for roped parties. A few rock steps

The top of the narrowing gully of Easy Terrace

The scrambles on B-Buttress culminate in a rocky arête

require care. A short walk along a pleasant rocky ridge leads to the summit.

Alternative finish by the climbers' descent

This is more difficult but has more rock than the preceding finish. There is a well-trodden path if you find the correct way. From the left end of the level path at the top of B-Buttress Lower Section take the line of least resistance up walls and ledges going diagonally left above the steep rocks of B-Buttress Upper Tier to reach the crest of the buttress which is followed to the top.

There is a fine walk along the ridge of Dow Crag to Goats Hause and Coniston Old Man, or an easy return left along the ridge over Brown Pike to the Walna Scar track.

80. Easter Gully and Intermediate Gully

Grade 4 SD264977

A serious route where **a helmet and rope are advised**. The first section is a climbers' descent route. The crux of Easter Gully **is strenuous and forbidding**. 130m of height is gained.

This is a climber's scramble up the middle of Dow Crag in impressive rock surroundings. In all but perfect conditions it is unbelievably green and greasy.

Approach: Easter Gully is the deepest V-shaped gully in the centre of the crags, just right of the narrow, squat D-Buttress and left of the broad, broken E-Buttress. See diagram, Route 79.

Route: Scramble into the base of the greasy gully and struggle past a small chock into a bay below a huge impressive wedged block. This forms the crux of the route and needs a bold layback move around the left side of the block to reach The Amphitheatre below a steep pear-shaped crag, which has several classic rock climbs. Scramble left up a slanting line of flakes across a steep wall into the top of a chimney and onto the end of Easy Terrace (which constitutes the alternative climbers' descent route left). Go left along this to the first major gully above. (If you go further left you join the preceding scramble). This is the upper part of Intermediate Gully (the lower half is a severe and strenuous climb). Ascend the gully, which has a couple of small pitches, to the top.

81. E-Buttress

Grade 4✷ SD264977

This is a large rambling buttress on the right of the popular climbing area and contains a lot of grassy ledges and steep walls. There are several ways up, some of which incorporate some easy rock-climbing pitches, but the route described makes a logical scramble and is fairly well trodden.

Approach: From the rescue box go right under the toe of the slabby C-Buttress and the steeper, squat D-Buttress to Easter Gully, a deep gully with a chockstone in its lower part and a steep rock amphitheatre above. E-Buttress is on the right. See diagram, Route 79.

Route: Walk up broken ground to the start of Easter Gully, to below the jammed chockstone. Go on a grassy rake trending right to a ledge below a steep corner. Continue on the grassy rake to the right to a rock gully, which has an awkward exposed start. Continue more easily to the crest of the buttress.

Make a way up grassy ledges rightwards to an awkward rock step in the gully. Climb its right wall on good holds, then rocks on the right to a grass neck. Cross to a grass recess in the gully on the right and climb out by a scoop on the right. The easiest route now crosses onto the bigger gully on the right and then gains the spiky arête on the right to reach the summit ridge.

A more difficult and direct finish can be made directly up from the scoop, by a difficult exit onto grass, whence a zigzag route leads up left to the buttress crest.

From below this appears a formidable scramble, but is mainly an unsatisfactory ascent of grass ledges. **Rock requires care. There is a serious atmosphere as the route feels quite big with few escapes. Rope advised.** 140m of height is gained.

A route with more continuous rock keeps to the left side of E-Buttress, overlooking Easter Gully. This is **Route 1** (grade 4) first ascended in 1886 by W.P. Haskett-Smith and J. Robinson in the rain!

82. F-Buttress

Grade 4 SD264978

This is a route with a mountaineering feel about it.

Approach: At the right-hand end of the crags is the deep wide North Gully, capped by overhangs. On its right is a narrow spur, which provides the route. See diagram, Route 79.

A steep section poses a rock-climbing problem for a short distance. The rock is vegetated and loose in places. Care is required and **a rope is useful** for the route's crux. 140m of height is gained.

Route: Start to the right of a small subsidiary gully where the rocks protrude in an easy spur. A spiky rib leads to a grass platform below a rock wall. Climb this close to the gully and continue more easily to where the spur abuts against a wall. The nose above is impracticable. Move down the grass slope to the left for 12m to a steep grassy crack, which breaks awkwardly through the rock barrier. A grassy groove is taken to a stance in an overhung chimney. Escape left onto easy ground where one can regain the ridge on the right by an awkward and exposed step. (The whole of the steep barrier can be avoided by an excursion into the gully on the right). Rocks above give a choice of ways to a final easy broken ridge to the summit.

DUDDON VALLEY

The gentle beauty of the Duddon Valley is typical of Lakeland scenery at its best. It is an inspiring blend of colourful woodland, rock outcrops and rough fell, with a backdrop of higher fells to round off the scene. There are no major crags, no major villages and only a narrow tortuous road traverses the valley floor. It remains the least spoilt of the Lakeland valleys and offers a peaceful sanctuary from the more popular centres.

Some of the best scrambling is centred on the little side valley of Seathwaite and the craggy end of Crinkle Crags which overlooks the head of the Duddon. The rock is generally firm, rough and clean. The sunny aspect and attractive views makes a good recipe for an enjoyable outing.

There is a campsite at Turner Hall Farm, near Seathwaite.

Car parking and transport

Parking is generally easy to find, the most popular being Birks Bridge car park. There is no suitable public transport. (The postbus is impractical.)

THE SEATHWAITE VALLEY

This attractive side valley bites into the back of the Coniston Fells. Seathwaite Tarn, a small reservoir, is cradled between craggy slopes, with Great Blake Rigg dominating the head of the lake. Tarn Beck leaves the reservoir then runs in a broad boggy area before tumbling in lively cascades over craggy slopes to a gentler valley and the junction with the Duddon near Seathwaite. In its lower half the Seathwaite valley is separated from the Duddon by a low rocky spine, the Troutal Tongue.

The following scrambles are described in a logical sequence, and can be combined to create a great day out, particularly if the summit of Greyfriar is included for its excellent views over the central fells of Lakeland.

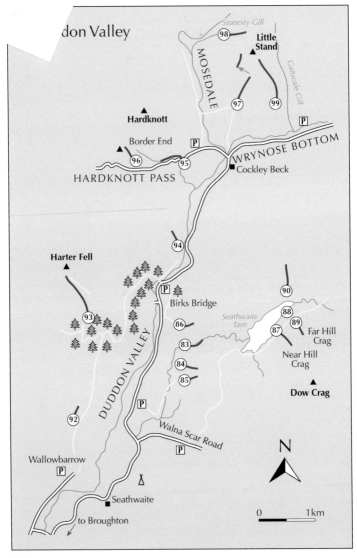

don Valley

Stonesty Gill

MOSEDALE

Little Stand ▲

Gaitscale Gill

98

97   99

Hardknott ▲

Border End

▲   P

96   95   WRYNOSE BOTTOM

HARDKNOTT PASS   ■ Cockley Beck

94

Harter Fell ▲

P

93   Birks Bridge   _Seathwaite Tarn_   90

88

86   87   89 Far Hill Crag

83

84   Near Hill Crag

DUDDON VALLEY   85   **Dow Crag** ▲

92

P

Walna Scar Road

P

Wallowbarrow
P

N

Seathwaite ■

to Broughton

0   1km

TARN BECK AREA

83. Tarn Beck

Grade 1 or 2 according to choice ****** *SD239984*

Approach: The best approach is from a parking place at SD 231975, about 400m past a cattle grid on the valley road where it rises around High Tongue, 1½km north of Seathwaite. From this parking place take the left-hand path which descends towards Tarn Beck and turns up the valley through woods. Keep left of a building and go through a gate to a footbridge over the stream. Other tracks up the valley converge here. The scrambles on Throng Close Buttress and Crag Band Buttress are seen above. A very wet area is crossed continuing upstream to another footbridge where the stream is entered to reach the foot of the first cascades.

The stream has twin channels and runs down a broad open course. Scrambling can be varied at will, so choose how easy or wet to make it. 60m of height is gained.

Route: Start in a broad bowl before a wide rock wall with waterfalls at either side. Gain the easy-angled rib between and go past a small spear-like pinnacle. There is an arête on the right of a small middle overflow channel. Gain this from the left and climb it with hands on the sharp crest. The angle eases to another broad basin. The main right stream takes a bouldery course. Either take this if it is dry, or the rocks at its side. Now there is a choice; the left channel is most interesting if dry, or else take the easy slabs of the right stream. Reach the point of divergence of the two streams.

The character changes and the single stream issues from a v-cleft. Enter this from the left, climb up a little to avoid a steep wall above a pool but immediately swing down good holds to the streambed and continue up slabs on the left of a waterfall. Above is a grassy shelf with crags on the left. A nice finish is up a small spur on the left (easier than it appears) by a series of flakes, with a step left at the top. Or take the easier angled slabs a little further upstream, again on the left bank.

A cascade near the top of Tarn Beck

You can continue to Seathwaite Tarn (Routes 87–89) and Great Blake Rigg (Route 90), or walk a short way left (north) to reach a path which drops to the intake wall gate below Little Blake Rigg to incorporate the fine scramble up this rock (Route 86).

There are two other good scrambles on the rocks to the right of Tarn Beck and these are described below.

84. Throng Close Buttress

Grade 1★★ SD240982

This and Route 85 are on the rocky slopes south of Tarn Beck, overlooking the narrow spine of Troutal Tongue. They are easy to access and are located in a quiet, unspoiled area.

Approach: Follow the directions as for Route 83, Tarn Beck, from the parking at SD 231975 to the first footbridge, where the crags come into view just past the wood. Then cross marshy ground to an old track, left of a prominent pine to reach the foot of the lower rock cone

A pleasant broken scramble on impeccable rock. Escape is possible at most points. The height gain is 110m.

Throng Close and Crag Band

Slabs above the exposed step on Throng Close Buttress

of the left-hand buttress. The right-hand buttress is Crag Band Buttress.

Route: Start at the toe of the lowest pyramid, then move across to its stepped right edge which is climbed to its top. Walk right, across a grass shelf to the foot of a spur. There are large boulders below this. Go right, under an overhanging wall, then back left on its top passing a rock shelf. Make an exposed step right, onto another shelf and gain slabs above on the left. (An easier, less exciting way climbs grooves on the left side of the spur). Now keep to the crest of the buttress to reach a more level section, then go over the right-hand of two perched blocks. This emerges on a grass rake, with the continuation of the ridge on the left. Climb the steep wall close to its edge, about 3m left of a heather groove, using big flaky holds. The ridge continues at an easy angle, with some short, steep walls for interest.

Tarn Beck (Route 83) is very close and a short descent allows it to be incorporated into the day's sport.

85. Crag Band Buttress

Grade 3✱✱ SD240981

This is the right-hand, slightly steeper buttress next to Throng Close Buttress.

Approach: Follow the directions as for Tarn Beck (Route 83) to the footbridge over the stream. Cross a stile on the right to join a track which winds up through two gates whence a traverse of the bracken slopes takes you left to the foot of the buttress. See diagram, Route 84.

A slabby buttress, exposed in parts, but with good holds. **Rope advised for the first section, difficult.** 80m of height is gained.

Crag Band Buttress gives a difficult scramble on excellent rock

Route: Start at the toe of the buttress close to a stone wall. Clamber up to a holly bush. Go under it to the right and up a grassy groove at the side of a huge flake. Come back left along a ledge to clean rocks above the holly to slabs and a thin arête, climbed on its right side along a thin diagonal crack (quite good holds). The arête continues with a fine slab on its left side, which appears a formidable problem. However, go a few feet left and climb the side of the slab at a little crack by a block. This leads easily to the top. Go right, up past a block, to another ledge with blocks. Move right again, and climb an awkward little corner to the top of the steep section. Past a grassy gap the ridge rises again on slabs. Cross over to the right and climb a speckled slab just short of the arête. Now an easy-angled rock crest rises to a final tower.

It is easy to find further scrambles in this area, either by descending further left to Tarn Beck (Route 83) and Little Blake Rigg (Route 86), or continuing to the scrambles around Seathwaite Tarn (Routes 87–90).

86. Little Blake Rigg
Grade 2✱✱ SD241990

Pleasant, clean rock with airy scrambling. Although there are some difficult sections, the route is easier than it appears. 100m of height is gained.

Well to the left of Tarn Beck is a line of broken crags that has a steep, light-coloured crag (Burnt Crag) high on its right side. Left of this is a broken buttress with a conspicuous white quartz streak in the gully to its left. The route winds a way up this buttress of excellent rock.

Approach: Park at Birks Bridge car park. Go left on the road a few yards then take a level path right, through the forest, almost to rejoin the road. Over a stile, go up and over the fell rise, where the route can be easily identified. Cross a boggy hollow and mount right to a hidden gate in the wall. Through this cross the bracken slope left to the lowest rocks.

Little Blake Rigg, location

Route: Start at the foot of a small rock spine (there is a cairn here), with an awkward step right at its top. Above on the left is a nose with a small, perched block. It is most easily climbed just on the right to gain a groove. Continue to a large grass shelf below a fine buttress. Start near the right edge, but move left then back right to cross a mossy slab on the exposed edge. Continue to a grass ledge, which leads right into a corner. Cross a grass platform back left to the edge and slant up easy rock on the crest to a steep tower.

Little Blake Rigg

Scrambling on Little Blake Rigg

Avoid this on the left and climb the delicate slabs in an exposed position left of the quartz-streaked gully.

The hillside above is a jumble of small outcrops, but it is more interesting to incorporate the more continuous rocks on the right above the steep climbers' wall of Burnt Crag, reached by a short descent. There is a clean rib in the facing wall and this is climbed to a grass ramp slanting right. Clean rocks of an easy rib fade into the fell. Beyond a grassy gap a little tower can be climbed direct to provide a good finale with a rocky summit.

To reach the further scrambles contour round the craggy slopes to the right with little loss of height to reach Seathwaite Tarn.

SEATHWAITE TARN

The setting is peaceful and acts as a reminder that it is easy to find both beauty and solitude on the busiest of summer weekends. The following routes lie on the south-east side of Seathwaite Tarn where crags tumble to the lake shore. A small path traverses well above the lake.

87. Shudderstone How and Near Hill Crag
Grade 2 NY255987*

Seen from the dam, Shudderstone How is the prominent knoll which rises out of the water about half-way along the lake.

Approach: Park on a small lane that forks right (signed to Walna Scar) about half a mile past Seathwaite. After half a mile, turning right at a fork, park just through the fell gate. Take the waterworks road, left through a gate, and follow it rising gently to the dam at the outlet to Seathwaite Tarn. A slight path goes around the right side of the lake to cross

Excellent rough rock, but it becomes **very slippery when wet**. The route links the most attractive pitches on the crag and, although devious at times, is quite interesting. **There are two** →

← **difficult sections where a rope may be useful** – one low down, the other high up. The height gain is 150m.

the col at the head of Shudderstone How. Leave the path before this and drop to lake level to pass below one rib to another out of sight of the path. Start at a rock outcrop at water level. There is a cairn here.

Route: Go leftwards up the slab to a steep exit. Continue up easier rocks overlooking the edge on the right. At its top descend grass to the base of the main sweep of slabs just to the right. The front of this makes a fine difficult pitch, cairn. Climb a grass groove for 3m then go up the rib on the right. Step onto a grass ledge (right) and regain the rib, which gives excellent scrambling to a mossy slab. At a flat grass platform go up a clean prow in the centre of the bay to the top of the How.

In the gap is a large square boulder. Mount the slab behind this and walk left to the right end of a steep wall above boulders. Climb the right-hand block by thin twin cracks. Keep left on the edge of the rock to a grass platform. Ascend the next slabs up the middle to a point

Shudderstone How and Near Hill Crag

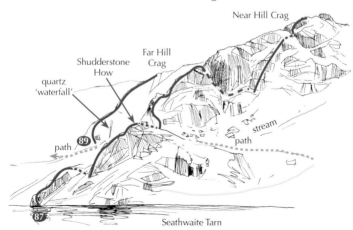

Seathwaite Tarn

Slab scrambling on Shudderstone How

below a steep, slabby wall, which is beyond the scope of scrambling. An unsatisfactory messy route can be made left of the steep rocks but a far more interesting, though devious, route is as follows.

Descend the short gully on the right to the base of the steep rocks. (This point can be reached with less interest from halfway up the slabs along a terrace.) Walk well to the right below the steep crag past a mossy section, to more amenable rocks and a cairn. Climb a clean rib to a steeper wall and escape right to rocks on the side of a grassy gully and back left. On the right a sweep of quartz-flecked slabs lead on. Where they peter out, move left onto more slabs and walls. Near the top move left along a grass ledge to a good steep rib. Above is a prominent steep prow with a bulging block at its foot. This section is exposed and a safety rope may be useful. From the base of the block move right along an airy ledge and climb up to a grass platform. Move back left onto the arête with some suspect rock in an exposed position. Follow the edge to the top.

Goat's Hause is an almost horizontal walk across the fell to the left.

88. Raven Nest How

Grade 2✱ SD258991

Steep and exposed but perfect rough rock with good holds. 25m of height is gained.

The next steep knoll near the head of the tarn looks formidable but yields a very short little gem.

Approach: As the Route 87, but continue along the path and drop to the lake level.

Route: Start at the right-hand corner of the crag at a slab about 4m left of the edge. The first 4m is quite tricky but soon eases. Move right to the edge and gain a grass ledge.

Raven Nest How

Step steeply back left onto slabs and left a few feet into a steep corner. Climb this up the side of a detached block. An exposed ledge leads horizontally left to the front. Finish by rocks on the left of the arête.

Raven's Nest How gives a short steep scramble.
Photo: G.Dewitt

179

89. Far Hill Crag
Grade 2✹✹ SD258988

Good rough rock in a succession of steep walls. 50m of height is gained.

This lies above Raven Nest How (Route 88) and is the logical continuation of that route. On the right side of the crags is a prominent quartz band, which from a distance looks like a thin cascade. This ribbon is unattractive for scrambling, but an excellent route starts a little below it.

Approach: Either continue a short way on the path which crosses Shudderstone How or, after Route 88, Far Hill Crag is seen above the path. See diagram, Route 87, for both.

Route: Start in a steep groove about 6m below a rowan, and step onto slabs on the left. Continue past the tree to the top of the first rib. On the left is a grass patch below the steep side wall of an arete. Go to the top corner of this patch to ascend a steep, cracked wall for 4m onto the arête. Follow a series of short, steep walls to a grass

The slab of strange whorls at the top of Far Hill Crag

Far Hill Crag

quartz 'waterfall'

terrace below a steep crag. Climb a subsidiary rib to gain slabs at a mossy recess, just left of the steeper crag. Above is a slab of strange whorls, which provide small but good holds.

90. Great Blake Rigg

*Grade 3** SD259994*

This impressive buttress lies on the slopes of Grey Friar and overlooks the head of Seathwaite Tarn. The crags have a steep left wall, but the crest rises in a series of buttresses set at a reasonable angle. The upper sections offer easier alternatives to the described route, which tries to maintain the interest of the first section.

Approach: By any combination of the preceding scrambles, or a walk up the waterworks road to Seathwaite Tarn. A triangular nose forms the lowest buttress, some overhangs providing a landmark. A preliminary scramble up a rib from a perched boulder can be incorporated to the terrace below the first buttress.

Exposed in places, with some free-standing flakes which require care and judgement. **A rope is advised** for security on key pitches which are **high in the grade**. Avoid this route if the rock is damp. 150m of height is gained.

Great Blake Rigg

rock climbs

prelim

1 – 4 Sections

Route: Start below and right of the prominent line of overhangs, where a deep right-facing crack splits the crag. Gain the flaky crack from the right and climb it strenuously for 2m or avoid it by another detour on the right wall, then move left onto a rock platform. Continue up for 6m to a ledge below a steep wall. Slant right up the ledge then back left to less steep rock. This is now right of and level with the overhangs. A good slab above is gained by a steep step on the right, and a series of steps lead up the right edge to more broken ground at the top of the first section.

To maintain interest, walk along grassy ledges rightwards to reach the foot of the second section. This presents a broad slabby front. Start just past the left-hand corner, up easy rocks on the left of a grassy depression. After 15m, below a steep wall, move back right along a rock ledge above the grassy depression to reach the edge

Steep scrambling on Great Blake Rigg. Photo: M.Tedd

of the slabs. These give excellent scrambling to a shelf below Section No. 3.

Straight up is rather scrappy, so walk 50m left to where the buttress rises in a clean easy-angled well-broken slab. Climb the slab on good holds to a narrow horizontal heather ledge below a steeper, more vegetated part. Now traverse left onto mossy rocks with good holds partly hidden.

Above is Section No. 4, which has a very steep left wall with an overhung corner on its right. Just right of this corner is a leftward slanting groove, which provides our exposed route; there is an easier alternative on the rib to its right. Climb the left-slanting groove, step left at its top and traverse across the top of the overhanging groove to easily gain a grass ledge. A final slab leads to the open fell.

The nearby summit of Grey Friar is a fine viewpoint. To return to the parking at SD 231975 go down the water-works road from Seathwaite Tarn for 500m then at a waymark, branch right on a path which zigzags down past Crag Band Buttress to the footbridge over Tarn Beck.

91. White Pike

Grade 1 SD247953

Disjointed, but good in parts on generally good rock, although care is required in places. Height gain is 120m.

A little known summit for it is merely the end of the ridge south of the Walna Scar track, yet from the southern fringes of the Lakes its steep profile is quite distinctive.

Approach: About half a mile past Seathwaite fork right (signed to Coniston and noted as 'Unfit for cars'). Keep straight on at a junction and park through a gate at the start of the Walna Scar track. Follow the track until below the first quarry spoil heap where a green track slants right to a gate. Turn right on a horizontal track above the wall, past old quarry buildings. Fork left on a faint green track just past the spoil heaps and follow this round the hillside through a little gap with a fine seaward view. The path continues around the hillside and the crags soon come into view. The scramble takes what appears to be a long broken skyline ridge.

Route: When below the crags look for a prominent knob with an overhang below its top left edge. Below and left of this the best starting rocks are on a narrow rib which rises from a patch of bracken. Mount the edge of scree to its base. Climb shattered rock up the front to a grass ledge at 6m. Move left for 4m onto slabs and ascend these to a grass terrace.

You could continue directly, but a longer and more interesting diversion is to incorporate the prominent knob, which lies to the right. Descend to the very foot of this and climb a steep edge, moving left onto the rock edge where the angle eases. At the top go left across grass to another rock spur. Move onto the front by a small shelf then keep more or less to the crest of the spur, with odd steepenings and some walking before a definite steeper knoll is reached. Ascend by a groove in the middle and more shattered rocks to the top.

Descent can be made along the ridge towards Walna Scar, or alternatively drop left to the quarry, avoiding the old workings, which are dramatic in places. The ridge to the south of White Peak is quite shapely, and the pyramid of Caw and the sharp Stickle Pike are prominent.

92. Hollin How and Basin Barrow

Grade 2 SD221971

Two outcrops of good quality rock may be incorporated into a day on Harter Fell. Note that an obvious

Hollin How and Basin Barrow

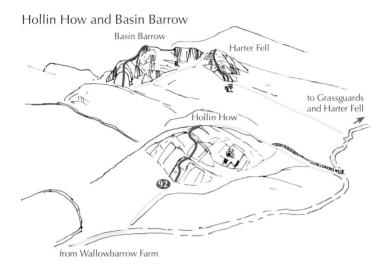

Basin Barrow

Harter Fell

to Grassguards
and Harter Fell

Hollin How

92

from Wallowbarrow Farm

Low outcrops of rough rock, supplied with generous incut holds, can be linked by rough walking to make a worthwhile diversion. 25m of height is gained on Hollin How and 30m (twice) on Basin Barrow.

preliminary scramble on the right edge of Wallowbarrow East Buttress suffers from a surfeit of heather.

Approach: A narrow lane on the west side of the river Duddon ends at Wallowbarrow Farm where parking is allowed in return for a voluntary donation. Past the farm turn left on a bridleway which mounts under the crags (popular with rock climbers). Soon after Low Stoneythwaite reach the open fell, and the low rocky hump of Hollin How is seen on the left across a boggy hollow.

Route: A clean, quartz-veined slab is the obvious way up Hollin How. Descend along the crest of the hump to regain the bridleway at a gate. Through this, mount the rough slopes to the right side of Basin Barrow. A clean thin slab, directly above a holly, and the following steps lead pleasantly to the top. Walk down a grassy rake below the steep central part of the crag to a fine slab

The slab of Hollin How

at the left end. Climb the centre of this, with increasing exposure, to more broken rocks. At a grassy trough climb the ridge to the right.

The scramble on Brandy Crag of Harter Fell (Route 93) can be seen ahead. Regain the bridleway, which continues past Grassguards into the Dunnerdale Forest. Join the approach to Brandy Crag at a road junction.

93. Harter Fell by Brandy Crag

Grade 2★★ or 3★★ by the Central Crag
SD223990

Good solid rock throughout. A scramble/walk with 300m of height gain. **Rope advised for the Central Crag start**.

A fine sunny way to the top of Harter Fell with a multitude of small crags providing excellent sport on good rock. The biggest crags lie at the start, with the obvious steep central rock of Brandy Crag providing the most difficult challenge. (Brandy Crag is a steep square-cut, castle-shaped outcrop just above the forest and a succession of

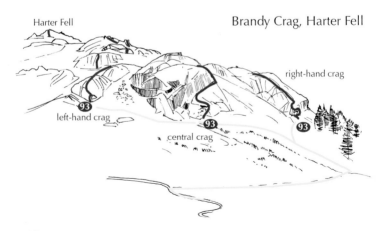

Harter Fell

Brandy Crag, Harter Fell

right-hand crag

93

left-hand crag

93

central crag

93

smaller craglets lead on to the summit.) More in keeping with the rest of the scramble is the right-hand crag. On the succeeding outcrops many variations are possible to suit your taste. Many scrambles can be devised but the one described here is probably the most continuous. The walking between is never more than a few minutes.

The difficult Central Crag start to Brandy Crags. A scrambler is near the top.
Photo: G.Dewitt

Approach: From the pleasantly situated riverside car park at Birks Bridge, take the forest road over the river and rise gently past Birks. A path forks right and rejoins the road. Take an uphill right fork and where the road doubles back the crag can be seen above the forest edge. At the next bend leave the road by turning right at a level path, to where it starts to descend close to the junction of old and new trees. Cross rough ground to reach the foot of the crags.

Route: There are **three ways to begin the scramble**.

1 At a similar grade to the rest of the route, the **right-hand crag** (grade 2, 50m) is composed of pleasant easy slabs reached by a steeper but interesting start. The steep base has a tree with flakes on its right. From the base of the tree circle right, around the flake, to gain the top of the tree, then pull on the next flake edge to enter the chimney it forms. Easier scrambling up the crest of the crag leads to its top. The next rocks are reached by traversing left above the central crag.

2 The **central crag** (40m) looks formidable face on, but an exposed grade 3 scramble is possible. A rope is advised. To the right of a slanting corner is a slab with heathery rocks at its foot. Start up the heathery rocks to a ledge with a block. Cross the slab delicately, heading diagonally left (below a heathery ramp) to easier angled rock below a steeper wall. A nut runner will protect the second here. Traverse right easily then step onto a higher ramp and go round the corner into a steep grassy gully. Climb this to reach easy ground.

3 The **left-hand crag** is much shorter and similar in grade to the right. A rib is climbed on its right side to gain a huge flake. Move left onto the nose, which soon eases in angle.

To continue: the next rocks lie directly ahead, above a fence. Left of a central bay is a fine clean slab which runs into a rib with a precariously perched block that is best avoided. Walk on to the next rocks. Aim for the lowest bouldery rocks on the left. Climb two large boulders to their exposed top whence a cracked slab makes a delicate finish. Immediately right is a grey block. Climb this left to right, to face a long low wall of crag ahead. Walk right 30m to below a twin buttress split by a bilberry gully. Mount the broad shelf to the right of the gully and continue up broken ribs.

The next small outcrop has a tiny pointed block at its foot. Climb directly from this then walk right to the foot of a steep skyline turret. A groove at the lowest point of this is climbed awkwardly. Ahead another low outcrop is best climbed at its left. Across an intervening dip lie the summit rocks. Join a path left towards the skyline outcrops. Start scrambling again at a rock tooth just by the path. After another slabby knoll, cross the slabs to the foot of the final rock tor (to the right of the trig point which is on a lower more accessible top). The most satisfying finish is by a crack, which splits the steep wall. This is much easier than it looks. Other alternatives abound.

94. Castle How

Grade 2 NY237004*

On the west side of the river, opposite Hinning House, is this isolated rocky knoll.

Approach: From Birks Bridge car park cross the river and follow a path upstream until at a stile the knoll appears ahead. In low water it is possible to boulder hop across from the common near Hinning House.

Route: The scramble follows the front of the buttress. There is a **choice of starts** either side of a steep barrier about 10m up. Start at the lowest rocks at a jumble of boulders.

Good scrambling, longer than it looks, with a sunny aspect. The steep bits are well furnished with positive holds. 40m of height is gained.

Castle How

The crux of Castle How scramble is steep with good holds.
Photo: G.Dewitt

1   The **Left-hand** start is easiest, heading up easy mossy rock to the left end of the steep lower barrier, which is climbed, then step right to a ledge on its top. Easy slabs lead to a grass platform below the steep upper wall.

2   **Right-hand** start. This is more in keeping with the steeper rock above. Climb easy, mossy rocks for 12m to the right side of the steep lower barrier, then move right to clean slabs on the right of a mossy gully. After 6m move right round the steep rib and up on good holds to a grass terrace. Climb a slab to the steep upper wall.

To **continue**, climb the steep upper wall about 4m right of the edge on good holds, then move right to incorporate a clean slab. The scramble continues a little past a grassy gap.

95. Hardknott Gill
Grade 1 NY238016 🌳🌳

Route: Start where the Hardknott Pass road crosses the gill on the Duddon Valley side. There is a good parking place below the bridge. Scramble up to the bridge, go through the culvert and continue up the narrow ravine. There are short stretches of rock scrambling interspersed with boulder hopping and walking. The ravine opens out and at a sharp right bend go out of the gill left to reach the road.

This pretty little gill provides a modest, easy scramble with a height gain of 100m. It can be combined with the scramble up Border End.

96. Border End

Grade 1 NY231016

This easy scramble on good rough rock is ideal as a continuation to Hardknott Gill, Route 95. 80m of height is gained. The summit of the Hardknott road pass is crowned by a large cairn, just below which, on the Esk side, is a small parking place. The scramble starts opposite this.

Route: Surmount a steep little wall then walk left towards a prominent rock spur with a steep right wall. Scramble up the front of this spur on lovely rough rock, by a succession of shelves and steps, to the summit plateau.

It is worth going to the far cairn overlooking Eskdale for the spectacular view across the valley to the Scafell peaks.

97. Little Stand

Grade 2✱✱ NY248026

A long scramble up 320m, on sound, rough rock with a wide choice of route. The route seeks out a succession of rock knolls. Described as grade 2, but sections are easily bypassed and there is scope for more difficult climbing variations.

The steep, rocky southern arm of Crinkle Crags drops into the head of the Duddon Valley overlooking Cockley Beck. The scope for scrambling is broad – another easier route is described on Red How (Route 99) on the eastern side of the mountain – but the following route takes a logical line with a minimum of walking between rocks and has a fine finish up the sharp rocks of Little Stand. A slight path follows the line of the scramble, but wends around the crags instead of up them.

Approach: Either park near Cockley Beck farm, cross the bridge, go over a stile on the right, across a tiny footbridge then strike up the fellside on a slight path to below the

Little Stand

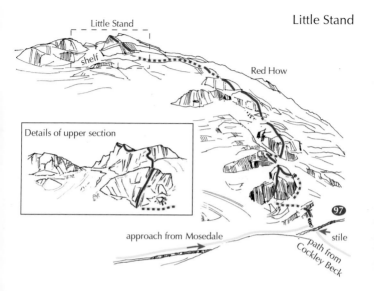

rocks; or, better, park a short way up the Hardknott road (where there is ample space) at the start of a path which traverses into Mosedale. Follow this path up the valley until level with the intake wall on the right. Cross the stream and keep above a fence to the foot of a prominent clean knott of rock on the skyline. The crag is just above a stile, where the direct path joins.

Route: Start at a rib directly above the remains of a low stone wall. This soon steepens into difficulties, which are best avoided on the right to climb the wall just right of a spike. The steep crag lies above. On the left of the main face is a heathery break. Slant up this from left to right, go past a steep block and left across a wall to a length of easier angled rough slabs to the top of the knoll. (An easier alternative gains the slabs by a ledge above a small ash half way up the right side of the crag.)

The summit pyramids of Little Stand

Continue up the next knoll, then cross a gully to rocks on its right. Climb the left side of a steep rib (or the slabs to its right) to the next knoll. A broad crag bars the way ahead. A scrambling route lies on the right past a grass ledge to reach an easy-angled rib which develops into slabs to the next top.

Walk to a small craglet which leads to a broad grass shelf, where the summit crags of Little Stand are well displayed. To follow the described route, walk left along the shelf where the pyramid-shape of the final rock is seen (see sketch).

Start this section above the grass shelf at the larger, slightly higher of two outcrops, at a central rib (cairn).

This crag is more continuous and exposed than anything preceding it. **Rope may be useful**. The rib leads into slabs slanting right, past a line of perched blocks, to a flat rocky platform which hosts a small pool in wet weather. Scramble above the right end of the terrace (a series of steep walls with good holds), first by a rib into a groove. Exit left round a block. The steep wall above is awkward.

Walk left to the foot of a pyramid of slabs and climb the front of these by a gangway. Finish easily round the rib left, or take a more difficult line up the steep front. Another pyramid ahead completes the route.

The walk along the almost flat summit ridge is very attractive, with rock outcrops mirrored in reedy pools: it is a fine way onto the Crinkles.

98. Stonesty Gill

Grade 2 or 3 NY246036

This cuts into the steep flank of Stonesty Pike and Little Stand, on the eastern side of Mosedale. The rock bed is very narrow, and unless it is a very dry spell will have too much water, which renders the trip useless.

Approach: There is parking up the Hardknott road from Cockley Beck at the start of the path into Mosedale. Follow the path well up Mosedale until almost opposite the gill. A track branches down towards a pool. Cross the boggy hollow and mount the steep slopes into the gill.

Route: The first significant obstacle is a double mossy fall; the lower part is easily climbed, the upper is more awkward on its left; then move into the middle to finish. The next landmark is a large, flat chockstone, which is passed on the left to reach the foot of the crucial grade 3 main fall. Start up rocks on the left and move up and right on good holds until a short awkward move leads to

In the right conditions it provides some entertainment. The crux pitch is serious with little protection on the exposed final difficulties. Individual bits are easily by-passed. Height gained is 130m.

The difficult pitch in Stonesty Gill.
Photo: G.Dewitt

a small ledge below the top of the fall. Take care with loose holds. Make a difficult and exposed move up using a good right- hand hold and small foot-holds to exit the pitch. This can all be by-passed by grassy ledges on the right. The gill continues easily to a green moss-covered chockstone, which is passed on its left. A final fall is bypassed then the gill followed until it peters out in the boggy plateau below the summit crags of Little Stand.

99. Red How from Wrynose Bottoms

Grade 1 or 2 NY255026*

Red How is the craggy, southern end of the Crinkle Crags ridge, overlooking Wrynose Bottoms at the head of the Duddon Valley. There is a lot of rock on a broad front; the route described takes a logical line up the right edge.

Approach: Park by the roadside in Wrynose Bottoms opposite Gaitscale Gill, a popular picnic spot. Take a path by the side of the gill, then cross a stile left and go

A long scramble with 320m of height gain, and some interesting sections but much of the route lies at a very easy angle. Good rock.

Red How

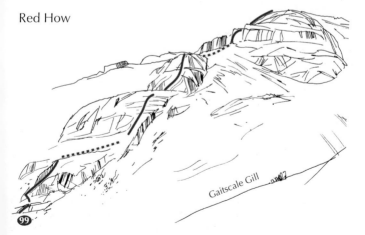

Gaitscale Gill

99

diagonally left over screes to the foot of the rocks. Start well below a prominent slab at the lowest outcrop.

Route: The first low wall is possible anywhere. A good start is by the left edge of a large flake.

The prominent slab with its grooved wall lies above. Mount slabs, which run left to right below the steeper left wall. Reach the foot of these by a left leading ledge. Climb the rough slab diagonally right, then straight up the centre of the buttress. At a flattish grass terrace go right to rocks overlooking the steep right wall. A mixture of rock walking and easy scrambling leads to a terrace below a more compact knot. Start at the lowest toe and climb clean rocks. A blunt rib gives delightful scrambling. After 12m move right onto more clean rocks.

Ahead, left of a grassy gully, is another slab outcrop. Start up light slabs then move left onto the main slabs. Walk on towards a steeper outcrop to the right of a grassy gully. Climb broken light coloured rocks to the base of a steep wall, which is more difficult than anything else on the route (grade 2). Easier alternatives exist on the left of the grassy gully. The route gains a groove in the centre of the vertical wall by a traverse from the left across an overlap. It is steep to start but there are good holds, an excellent pitch. The route now reverts to easy scrambling/rock walking up the right edge of the grass gully towards a prominent skyline tooth. Move left at the head of the gully to a terrace below a steep rock wall. Climb this by a series of steps trending right. The fine slabs left of the tooth are climbed by the left side of a large flake.

The summit cairn lies close and the flat-topped ridge gives a pleasant walk onto Crinkle Crags.

ESKDALE

A long, quiet valley of great charm, Eskdale can be split into two distinct parts: the lower gentle valley is a colourful mix of trees, bracken and heather entwining numerous rock outcrops on low fells; and the upper valley, a rugged, bare haven amongst the highest peaks of the area. The scrambling in Eskdale is especially varied with a fine mixture of crags and gills, and in Lower Eskdale some are composed of granite. The granite crags are often smoother with less holds than the more conventional Lakeland volcanic rock, yet still offer good sport. Otherwise, the rock is as good as anywhere in the Lake District – rough, sound and with plenty of holds. Upper Eskdale has several classic scrambles including the face of Ill Crag which is one of the longest in the Lakes. There is something of excellence to suit all tastes in Eskdale.

There are campsites at Fisherground (near Eskdale Green) and Hollins Farm, Boot.

Car parking and transport
At busy times the parking is inadequate and fills early although there are alternative small parking places along the narrow road running through the valley. There is no bus service.

LOWER ESKDALE

100. North-West Crags, Harter Fell
Grade 2✳ NY211001

The top half of Harter Fell on the Eskdale side is a tangle of dark, heathery crags which rise from a rough heather shelf. The route described has a mountaineering aura, as it winds an intricate way up a complex craggy hillside. It makes an excellent way up this interesting little peak, and the views are splendid over Eskdale to the Scafell range.

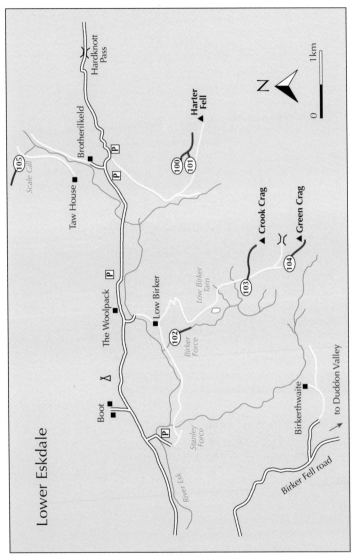

Lower Eskdale

Approach: Park above the cattle grid a little way up the Hardknott Pass road on the Eskdale side. Cross a small bridge and follow a rising bridle path. After passing Dodknott Gill it curves up onto the open moor. (This point can be reached by another path from Doctor's Bridge lower down the valley.) The old bridleway continues over a boggy moor towards the Duddon, but our path forks left towards the rocky pyramid of Harter Fell. Follow this, with another left fork, to the right-hand side of the rocks where a horizontal shelf runs below the crags. Go along this, past a line of overhangs to a heather gully which rises diagonally left. A further aid to identification, just past this, is a deep recess rising to a heather topped block and a short steep wall which contains a thin crack.

The scrambling is good in parts, easy and heathery in others, and much easier than first appearances suggest. Rock quality improves as height is gained although some parts stay greasy after rain. Height gained is 140m.

Route: Start in the easy gully and follow a slight path up the grass until above a heather topped pinnacle on the left (a useful check that you are on the route). Nearly 7m above the pinnacle leave the grassy gully in favour of the slabs; head along a ledge which traverses left to the front. Easy-angled rocks then lead to just below the top of the grassy rake. Now take heathery walls and ledges on the right, heading towards a steeper jagged wall on the skyline. Well below this at a horizontal shelf; move right to reach the cleaner, sunnier rocks of the buttress crest. Climb to the steeper rocks, first by a greasy groove, then

North-West Crags, Harter Fell

heather-topped pinnacle

upper crags

The Beanie

path to summit

100   101

Both the scrambles on the North-West Crags of Harter Fell finish up slabs on the upper crags

make an exposed traverse right, to the edge. Continue up easier angled rocks on the spur. A pointed perched block on the skyline is a landmark. Reach it by way of a steep rock nose, or easy ledges on the left. The block is on a fine little arête which levels into a crocodile spine and ends at a large shelf below the upper crags.

For maximum entertainment ignore the scrappy rocks above and complete the scramble by the route described below, which takes attractive rocks up the prow of the **upper crags**, the best scrambling on the route. Walk a short way below the crags on the right and descend to its lowest point under a steep wall. There is a detached flake block on its right. Climb the right-hand side of this block to gain a slabby ramp which ascends the edge of the steep side wall. Follow this to its top, step right and climb a final sweep of attractive slabs.

The summit of the fell is about ¼ mile away and is composed of two rock tors which provide a fitting finale.

101. The Harter Beanie

Grade 2✳ NY211000

This is a route up the clean rocks of the right edge of the north-west crags, incorporating a prominent hat-shaped knob, to finish by the upper rocks of the previous route.

Approach: As for the previous scramble (Route 100) to the right-hand side of the rocks where a horizontal shelf runs below the crags.

Pleasant scrambling on good, rough rock, seeking the most sporting way up a succession of outcrops. 140m of height is gained.

Both the scrambles on the North-West Crags of Harter Fell finish up slabs on the upper crags

Route: Near the right end of the crags, just right of the lowest point of smooth slabs, climb diagonally right on easy-angled rocks immediately left of a heathery groove. Climb over a block in the groove. Continue 6m under a steep side wall to a break. Climb the break and move diagonally left to the left side of a rib then left again to mount rock just before reaching heather. Reach a shelf below the Beanie. The centre of a subsidiary slab leads to the main knob which offers several ways. The prow offers a rock-climbing problem. It is recommended that you start about 2m right of the block at the base of the prow, climb right onto a ramp then steeply on good holds to the top of the Beanie. Across the grass neck mount a short slab and head for a slab above with a distinctive pale band.

A sporting ascent is to start 6m down to the left to make the most of a pleasing airy slab. Pull steeply onto the slab then climb up the steep prow to the top of the pale band, or finish more easily further left. The scramble fizzles out above so descend a grassy gully 10m left to incorporate more slabs. A left slanting heathery break leads onto steep frontal slabs; keep rising left (it is delicate but holds keep coming) to gain a heather ledge. More slabs lead onto easier ground. Keep on the rib as the angle eases to a junction with the previous route. The fine **upper crags** on the right provide the best finish (Route 100), by a slabby ramp on the edge of the steep side wall. See Route 100 for description.

102. Low Birker Force

*Grade 3** NY186002* ❦❦

Low Birker Force lies on the steep southern slopes of Eskdale, almost opposite Boot. This route is only feasible during a dry spell. The first half of the scramble lies up a broad boulder-floored streambed in a deep-cut ravine, its sides a profusion of hollyhocks. The imposing headwall, down which the force leaps and bounds, appears impossible but is climbed on its left side to escape on a hidden ramp below the final steep barrier.

Approach: Parking, for a fee, is often allowed at the Woolpack Inn half a mile past Boot. Just before the Woolpack Inn a lane branches right to Penny Hill. Cross the fine old Doctor Bridge and go right on a rough lane to Low Birker. Just past the buildings fork sharp left on a

The rock is granite, solid in the main, but care is required in places. The main pitch is very exposed and **a rope is advised**. The scramble is best done in low water, and note the rock is slippery where wet. **Avoid if at all greasy** – the rock takes a long time to dry. 110m of height is gained.

On the long crux section of Low Birker Force

lesser lane, one of Eskdale's old peat roads. Above the plantation, go right to a gate at the second wall. Go right along the wall side to enter the gill.

(Alternative parking can be found further down the valley at Dalegarth Falls. See the following scramble for description.)

Route: A short defile is followed by a chaotic jumble of boulders, large and small, which constitute the river bed. At a steep cascade climb a clean 9m rib on the left. Round the corner the formidable headwall comes into view. Scramble easily to the foot of the main falls and the start of the serious scrambling. Climb a slabby ramp on the left by a steep awkward corner to an easing of angle. Go up a steep rib to a small tree and move right to a ledge. Move up steeply again then climb the left wall to a small tree. Traverse right to a ledge below the final cascade. A direct ascent of the steep slimy rocks seems improbable but an escape is offered by a grassy ramp left.

Join a path along the top of the scarp. For a return go left along this to reach an old zigzag pony track (the old peat road) which descends to Low Birker. Continuation scrambles on Crook Crag and Green Crag (Routes 103 and 104) are reached by going right, along the path above the force to follow the stream past Low Birker Tarn. The foot of the Great Whinscale ridge lies across the boggy hollow.

CROOK CRAG AND GREEN CRAG

These two small peaks, along with many subsidiary knobbles, form a striking rock ridge which rises from the boggy moorland of Birker Fell. Although of very modest height, they provide a surprising wealth of good scrambling on excellent rough rock. The Great Whinscale route on Crook Crag gives a scramble of 180m vertical height. Combined with a scramble on Green Crag, another 120m vertical height, this gives a very satisfying outing, useful when higher peaks are in cloud.

103. Crook Crag by Great Whinscale
*Grade 2** SD194991*

Seen from the Birker Fell road, Crook Crag is the left-hand, northerly peak of the two. The route more or less follows the skyline ridge then ascends The Pike by its right-hand ridge. The summits must be counted amongst the nicest rock peaks in the Lakes.

Crook Crag from Birker Force approach

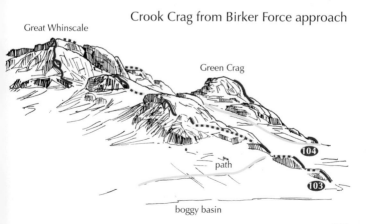

Great Whinscale

Green Crag

path

104

103

boggy basin

Crook Crag and Green Crag from Birker Fell road

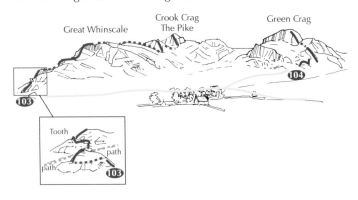

The scrambling seeks an interesting way up rock outcrops (exposed in places) – hence the grade of 2 – generally with plenty of choice. The holds are positive and solid, with only a few loose blocks, whilst friction is generally good. However, the coating of lichen renders the rock slippery soon after rain. Height gain is 180m.

Approach

1   Park along the minor branch lane (off the **Birker Fell road**) towards Stanley Force on the grass verge at the start of the private road on the right to Birkerthwaite, SD173980. Walk almost to Birkerthwaite and, where the lane turns towards the farm, continue straight ahead on the right of a wire fence and over a stile. Another stile ahead gives access to a boggy moss. Cross Smallstone Beck and continue along the flat moss (driest on its right edge). Fox Bield, a little rock island amongst the bog myrtle, is passed and the start of the scramble can be identified. A landmark is a small tooth-like protuberance on the lower skyline ridge. The route starts on rocks below and right of this. From the moss, mount a heathery rise and cross to the foot of the lowest rocks.

2   The same point can be reached **from Eskdale** by the old peat road from **Low Birker**, which mounts steeply onto the boggy shelf by Low Birker Tarn. The path crosses the scramble above the lowest outcrops.

3   The best approach of all is by the scramble up **Low Birker Force** (Route 102, grade 3). If you use the Dalegarth Falls car park, accessed by a narrow lane opposite the old school just before the rail terminus at Boot, there is a very attractive valley walk to Low Birker where the peat road is joined.

Easy scrambling on Great Whinscale

Route: The lowest rocks form a little knoll. Start up the right edge to reach a grass shelf. Walk left to rocks on the left edge. The next rocks are climbed on the right, by slabs to the left of a smooth slab. Cross the path. Mount a pile of blocks to a grass terrace and walk left to the tiny tooth. This is climbed direct, or a step left half way onto a little gangway gives more interest. Now take rocks above to a terrace. The small pillar ahead is easier than it appears and is climbed straight up the front on good holds. Another rock step above gains a broad terrace with a fine grey crag ahead – the most dominant feature of the scramble.

The grey crag appears formidable face-on, but the angle is reasonable and the scrambling is easy but airy. The route takes the clean rocks towards the left end of the face. Start on the right side of a triangular slab, then move right and up clean slabs above. The rocks steepen. Go to the base of a small overhang, then traverse right and up – or go left of the overhang, both ways give good scrambling. The good rock continues as a rib to a terrace. The short steep wall above is the most difficult part of the route; climb it straight ahead by a weakness which slants diagonally right. It is awkward to start, with a mantelshelf half way. Emerge on the ridge top.

There are numerous waves of rock along the intervening ridge, but the next real scrambling is on the summit cone of **The Pike**. Go right under the base of the rock pyramid to reach the right-hand arête. This slants leftwards to finish on a rock ridge to the summit. There is an easy descent down zigzag rakes on the right, or you can continue the scramble along the summit ridge down to a grassy col.

After another little hummock, descend to the broad col between Crook Crag and Green Crag. The summit of Green Crag can be reached by scrambling up the crags directly ahead, but a far more sporting route is provided by Route 104 which is reached by traversing below the crags. Descend from the col, and walk left below a long line of steep crags, past a grassy break to cleaner more amenable rocks just above a flattish area.

104. Green Crag, West Side

*Grade 1 or 2** SD197983*

Green Crag is the highest point on the southern end of the modest but rocky peaks which rise from the Birker Fell moor. Combined with a scramble on its neighbour, Crook Crag, it gives a fine day's sport. The described route takes a logical line with only short breaks between the crags. Many other ways can be found to suit all tastes.

Approach: As for Crook Crag (Route 103), go past Birkerthwaite to Smallstone Beck which is followed right to the foot of the crags. Aim for the lowest nose of rocks in a direct line with the summit, well right of a steeper band of crag. Alternatively, after doing the preceding scramble on Crook Crag (Route 103), descend the westerly slopes from the col before Green Crag to traverse below the

Excellent rough rock, best appreciated in dry conditions. Any difficulties are easily avoided, yet there is plenty of scope for grade 3 scrambling. 120m of height is gained.

Green Crag

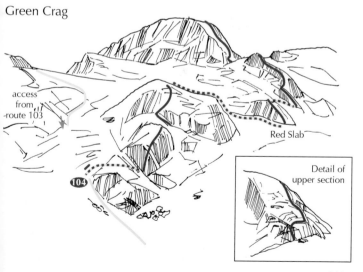

access from route 103

Red Slab

104

Detail of upper section

The summit rocks of Green Crag give good scrambling

steep wall of crags and reach the easier angled outcrops beyond a grassy break.

Route: Start at the foot of the rib above. (The lowest nose is too steep and dirty to enjoy and is best avoided on its left.) Start right along a sloping ledge then climb a rib to a grass terrace backed by a steep low wall. The easiest route is by slabs slanting left to a groove which leads through the steeper rock. Walk to the right, to the foot of a reddish slab, descending a short rock wall on the way. The right edge of the slab is good, but beware of a loose block. Walk right again, 30m, to slabs with a clutch of perched flakes at its foot. Mount the slabs leftwards then move 6m right to the rib (loose flake).

At the top of the knoll, the fine summit crags are revealed. There is a lot of steep rock, but the right-hand slabs are more practicable and much easier than face-on appearance suggests. They give a fine but exposed finish to the route. The start lies at the right side at a collection of boulders, where one rests upon another. Another feature is a grass ledge above the start, to the left of the slabs. Climb a blunt nose for 6m behind the boulders to just below the grass. Cross the steep edge right to gain the rough slabs and a ledge which runs right for 8m. Climb a slabby rib to a grass terrace. Ascend a steeper rib above then easy slabs to the top.

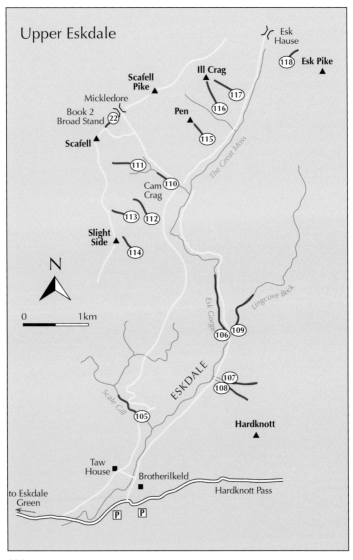

Upper Eskdale

105. Scale Gill (Cowcove Beck)

Grade 2★★ NY214024

Cowcove Beck drains the boggy moorland shelf between Scafell and Eskdale, becomes Scale Gill and joins the Esk half a mile above Brotherilkeld. This is an entertaining and easily accessible scramble that provides a sporting trip when poor weather rules out the higher fells. If you can criss-cross the stream you will enjoy a good scramble, even in poor weather, although the rock is slippery and care is required in such conditions (socks over trainers could be an advantage). The ravine is low walled with easy escapes almost anywhere. The width of the rock bed allows a good choice of route according to water conditions. In summer bracken encroaches on the edges of the gill. There are two impassable pools which detract from the continuity of the route.

The beck runs in an almost continuous little ravine floored with a solid rock bed which gives top quality scrambling up a series of cascades and pools. The rock is sound and well supplied with positive holds. 130m of height is gained.

Approach: Park either on the valley road verge before the start of the Hardknott Pass road, or 100m up the road, past the cattle grid. At the base of the hill take the rough lane towards Brotherilkeld, branching left just before the farm to a path by the river. Cross the footbridge to Taw House and go right along the bridle-path up the valley. After crossing several stiles a stone packhorse bridge is reached over the beck.

Route: The gill below the bridge is worth scrambling. Go through a gate just past the bridge and descend to the lowest rocks. The first real scrambling is a broad slab with the stream at its left-hand side, and another cascade is surmounted to reach the bridge. Pass under this to the first serious obstacle – a fine narrow cascade in the back of a dark recess, easier than appearances suggest. Start up the left-hand side of the first small cascade to a pool. Continue up slabs, left of the cascade to a slippery exit almost in the waterchute. If there is too much water, escape left a few feet lower and regain the stream above the fall.

The first obstacle in Scale Gill

The bed narrows into a defile with a slippery traverse on the steep right wall above a deep pool. Then reach a deeper pool with vertical walls backed by a steep fall, best avoided by an escape left, and regain the ravine about 30m above. The next fall is feasible on its right to finish up a central rib with a steep exit. After passing an opening the ravine begins again, with the first hazard passed on the left wall by a slimy slab, to a sharp bend. Then the going is easier heading to an ominous cascade above a deep circular pool. Escape left and regain the stream at the head of the cascade. Climb slabs on its left to a break in the gorge. Another broad deep pool lies ahead.

Reach the left-hand side and traverse just above the pool to a steep climb on good holds near the fall. The next pool is easiest climbed on the right. There is easier going for a while, always on a broad rock bed. Pass a side gully on the left to a little cascade, climbed on the right. The scrambling continues, always interesting, to a long narrow pool backed by a steep cascade, which can be avoided on its right or climbed close to the fall. Ahead is yet another cascade with fine slabs on its right to exit on the moor.

To return to the valley join the pack-horse track that lies just to the east. The scramble on Horn Crag (Route 114) provides a logical scrambling route to Scafell.

106. The Esk Gorge
*Grade 2*** NY227036* 🌿

Between the junction of Lingcove Beck and the Great Moss, the River Esk runs in a slight gorge of great beauty. A path traverses both its flanks well above the water, but walkers can only glimpse the many falls and pools. The lower end of the gorge opens out and is a very popular bathing and picnic spot on a warm summer's day. To traverse the bed of the gorge is Lakeland's finest major

The first section is open and the most interesting way must be sought, but later it develops into a more intimidating ravine where there is no escape for a while. Some of the traverses above deep water seem formidable at first glance, but prove reasonable. 140m height is gained.

stream expedition, both sporting and scenic and on perfect rock. The river normally carries a strong flow, which runs off slowly, fed by the broad sponge of the Great Moss. If there is too much water it is impossible to traverse round the pool edges and more time is spent out of the gorge than in. During a dry spell, however, the route's excellent rock and deep green pools make an attractive combination. Best done on a hot day in shorts, as there are several places where a brief, thigh-deep wade is necessary.

Approach: Park at the foot of Hardknott Pass, either a few hundred yards above or below the Brotherilkeld lane end. A path bypasses the farm to follow the river for a while, before rising through pasture and up the broad valley to the shapely pack-horse bridge at the confluence with Lingcove Beck.

Route: Just above the packhorse bridge is an impassable pool. Gain the rock bed of the right bank just above the bridge by a grass shelf. The first difficulty is a prow,

The initial difficulty in the Esk Gorge

rounded at water level followed by a steep ascent to a ledge. (Or gain the ledge more easily on the right.) Traverse a damp recess, and climb close to the fall. This completes the initial cascades and a short walk leads into a verdant ravine and a fine pool, backed by an attractive fall. Go around the left side and ascend the rocks through a narrowing to emerge at a broad pool and a 10m waterfall. The rocks of the right wall make an attractive pitch. Pass the next pool by a ledge on the right and go up a steep groove with good holds.

The angle is easy for a while but the broad rock bed provides good sport if you search for it. Make a fun crossing of the stream at a corbel. Cross to the left side of the stream just before the next narrowing. Gain the central rocks and go up a groove at the right-hand end of the next steep wall. Cross the stream again with care onto a central block. Cross back right at the lip of a pool to climb a steep flake crack with a small tree. Descend a rib to the exit of a deep pool and go up a steep rib on the other side onto grass. Regain the solid rock bed above. A small circular pool is best passed by a thigh-deep wade on its left side. Mount the left rib at the top – or cross to the right and up a flake crack. Climb the left rib of the next pool to open rocks; gain the central rocks. At the end of this is a bold leap across a deep channel and a tricky rising ramp on the block above. At the top cross to the slabby right wall.

The next pool is impassable and is avoided on the right. Regain the bouldery streambed. The ravine becomes deeper and more forbidding. Darker, mossier rocks add to the atmosphere. Easy scrambling along the left side leads to a long, deep pool backed by a fall. Traverse the mossy right wall with surprising ease to a more delicate ascent at the side of the fall. Cross the stream left onto a rib. Wade a short pool to gain the mossy slabs of the right wall. It is easier for a while before another longer wade along the left side of a steep-walled pool. Climb onto a ledge at its end and follow this above a deep pool, with an awkward little descent. Still on the left wall, the next pool is conquered by a serious traverse

An exposed traverse above a deep pool in the Esk Gorge

of a steep shattered wall, starting with a slight descent from a jutting block onto a rising traverse. Gain a shelf. This traverse proves much easier than first appearance suggests. Traverse slabs to a house-size boulder which blocks the ravine. Climb the short steep crack at its side to end the serious section.

A sting in the tail is provided by the final fall. Traverse mossy rocks on the right edge of a pool. The shelving rocks close to the fall are more difficult than anything else on the trip and most people will paw the rock then retreat a few feet to escape up the flank to end a satisfying expedition.

There is a choice of good scrambling continuations in Upper Eskdale, perhaps best for climber/scramblers is to take advantage of low water conditions which allow an ascent of the Esk and to continue up the demanding direct ascent of Cam Spout (Route 110).

107. Great Gill

Grade 2✱ NY227029

This is the best of the minor gills along the side of Eskdale. Although not comparable to the quality of its near neighbours, the Esk Gorge and Lingcove Beck, it makes a novel approach to the humble craggy summit of Hardknott. The continuation of the scramble on isolated crags set in a lonely, boggy plateau, is quite worthwhile, as it is on excellent rough rock.

Approach: As for the Esk Gorge (Route 106), walk up the gentle valley path from Brotherilkeld. The steep right-hand side of the valley has a craggy rim (note the isolated pinnacle of the Eskdale Needle high up). Well past this is a crag with two gills cutting through the hillside. The left-hand one is the scramble, about half a mile below the packhorse bridge over Lingcove Beck.

A surprisingly rocky gill which rises in a series of steps and small ravines. Unfortunately the main ravine is impassable. The route is best done in a dry spell when the rough rock can be used to the full. 150m height is gained on the gill.

Route: The gill becomes rocky about 45m above the valley track. The first feature is a 12m recess, climbed up the stream to bridge up a mossy exit. Two rough slabs follow with a steep traverse left near the top. Another steep recess is climbed on its left but a more serious obstacle above is best avoided altogether. Easier scrambling leads into a defile, where a cascade is passed by steps on the left. Enter a shady ravine guarded by trees. A long mossy rib steepens – keep to rocks on the left side, though it is awkward mid-way and steep at the top. This is only feasible in a dry spell. Climb a slab to below a prominent tree, through a slight ravine into a deeper ravine. This culminates in a steep, slimy runnel and is impassable. Abandon the stream at this point and walk up its edge. Take the higher of two grass rakes across the crags on the left. Near the top of the rake climb the rocks on the right, by a rib on the left of a prominent V-corner.

The mountain summit lies over to the right and several attractive craglets can be climbed on the way. The first is a knoll reached across the head of the stream. Climb the slabs at the right-hand end of the knoll, starting at the foot of a blunt rib. Climb slightly right up rough, clean slabs with plenty of holds to a slight ramp right. A prow above a grass ledge is climbed on its left side – an excellent pitch. Walk to the next knoll on the right, which has a fine sweep of slabs on its front. Climbers could devise satisfying pitches at various standards but a scrambling route exists on the right where a diagonal rib lies just right of a bilberry groove at the edge

Craglets above Great Gill

107

224

of the slabs. Climb the rib right to left, with an exposed step onto smaller continuation ledges, to reach the top of the bilberry chute. Finish up slabs on the right. Further small outcrops lie between here and the summit over to the right.

108. Bursting Gills

Grade 3∗ NY225029

Parallel to and very close to Great Gill, this deceptive gill starts as a very easy open stream and becomes progressively more interesting. This gill is similar in quality to, but quite different from, its neighbour Great Gill.

Approach: As for Esk Gorge (Route 106) and Great Gill (Route 107) but is 100m before Great Gill.

Route: After a tame start, enter a deep narrow cleft with a steep short exit. More open streamway follows to a small deep pool at the foot of a band of crags. The character of the gill changes above. Traverse around the pool and climb the stepped cascades in the narrow ravine. This is quite easy at first but a steeper 4m tier proves tricky; it is best on the drier left side. The gill lays back a short way before steepening again. A second awkward pitch is reached which is taken on mossy rock to the right of the cascade. Watch out for large loose blocks! The gill again flattens and a fork is reached. Take the main streamway on the left and another rift-like passage is entered which contains two more steep mossy pitches leading to the top.

The gill ends in the area of outcrops of sound rough rock described in Route 107. Alternatively a walk right along the rim of the plateau will take you to the Eskdale Needle, a fine pinnacle.

The upper reaches lie in a narrow ravine. Excellent rock, interesting situations with 150m of height gain.

109. Lingcove Beck

Grade 2✱✱ *NY227036*

A fairly narrow, shallow ravine with escapes possible anywhere, with deep pools, short falls and good rock to give interesting sport. The stream can carry a lot of water. The height gained is 100m.

An expedition of great beauty best achieved after a prolonged dry spell. Despite some disjointed scrambling due to impassable falls, it is quite worthwhile if only to enjoy the fine stream scenery.

Approach: Park at the foot of Hardknott Pass in Eskdale, follow the farm lane to Brotherilkeld, where a track leads up the broad flat valley to a pack-horse bridge over Lingcove Beck at its confluence with the Esk.

An alternative approach can be made from the Duddon side of Hardknott; park near the foot of the pass where a path traverses the hillside into Mosedale. Cross a low col at the head of Mosedale and descend the side of Lingcove Beck to the packhorse bridge.

Route: Start above the first impassable fall. Traverse awkwardly on the left wall or boldly jump the boulders to gain the pool below another fall to bypass the cascade on its left. Keep left on rocks past the next fall to an attractive diagonal spout into an almost enclosed circular pool. Climb the exposed stepped rib which forms the right edge of the pool to the top. Regain the gill where the stream is split by a central block. Creep round the right edge of the pool to the neck behind the block and make a bold step across the water to gain a rock stairway. This completes the first steep section. A ravine starts just above and progress is interesting, criss-crossing the stream amongst delightful rock scenery. At a deep pool traverse a mossy shelf on the right wall to reach a jammed block by a fall. Go below the block and straddle the spout. Traverse the slabby right wall, above a deep pool, delicately for about 6m to a point where you can ascend mossy rocks onto a traversing line to the top of the three falls. Traverse the next pools on the left and pass a small step by a damp overhung slab. The main scramble ends just above this.

Further up the valley towards Bowfell, the stream develops into two more scrambling sections. Highly recommended is the other major scramble in the area, the Esk Gorge (Route 106), for if the water level is low enough for Lingcove Beck, then the Esk should be in condition too.

Scrambles in upper Eskdale are worth the long approach. Thor's Buttress and Pen, and Ill Crags are seen beyond the Great Moss

UPPER ESKDALE

110. Cam Spout
*Grade 3 Direct**★★** Grade 1 Indirect NY218058*

The stream of How Beck, which descends from below Mickledore and Scafell, tumbles down attractive cascades in a small rocky ravine to the flat grassy area around the Great Moss. A path zigzags close to the ravine but views into it are limited. The indirect route is a very inferior, soft option.

Approach: Cam Spout lies on the main path to Scafell from Eskdale, approached either by the valley route from

227

The direct route sticks as close as possible to the bed of the gill and poses **some rock-climbing problems in exposed situations. Rope advised.** The rock is excellent. The main waterfall pitch can only be achieved in dry conditions. Height gain is 100m.

Brotherilkeld or the higher level shelf from Taw House. The ideal approach is by the Esk Gorge scramble (Route 106).

Route: The **indirect route** is obvious; close to the right edge with divergence into the stream where the angle eases above the main fall.

The **direct scramble** starts with a traverse of the first pool and a tricky start to ascend the right wall. From the bed of the second pool ascend the right wall onto the

The serious main pitch of Cam Spout.
Photo: G.Dewitt

rocky edge of the ravine which is followed to join the path. Regain the streambed at an amphitheatre of red rocks down which the stream cascades. Make sure there is not too much water near the top before embarking on this long and serious pitch, which is only for the experienced climber/scrambler. Mount rock steps in the left corner of the cascades, awkward in places, to reach a sloping shelf below a steeper barrier. Go right to cross the water and descend the shelf to gain good holds on the right wall. This point can also be reached directly keeping right of the water. Climb steeply until the bed can be regained. Follow a trench on the right of the water, easier now, but still interesting. The angle lessens but the narrow gill gives good sport to open ground in the combe below the rocky south-west side of Scafell – which can provide a continuation scramble (Route 111) almost to the summit ridge.

111. Scafell – South-East Side, Greencove Wyke

Grade 3✱ NY214061

From the grassy combe above Cam Spout, Scafell appears as a shapely pyramid of jumbled slabby crags. There is a steep crag close to the summit and a continuous broad belt of slabs low down. An interesting scramble with a minimum of walking can be devised, with a choice of routes. The difficulties described could be bypassed.

Approach: Either use this as a continuation of the scramble up Cam Spout (Route 110), or walk up the path by Cam Spout into the combe and cross the stream to the lowest rocks just above the path.

Route: The lowest rocks are characterized by an overhung base on the right side. Start at clean slabs to the left of this, left of mossy slabs. At its top, walk right to a grass terrace leading right. Climb the first continuous

Open slabby scrambling on good rock, though the route is quite exposed and serious and difficult in parts. **Good route finding is required to avoid straying onto difficult rock. A rope is advised.** 250m of height is gained.

slabs above which lead to a terrace below more imposing slabs ahead, which form a steep and serious section of the route. There is a prominent overhang in the slabs at about half height. Gain a groove directly below this from the left. Climb it until below the first overhung recess, then bear left to the edge. Just round the corner is an exposed gangway which provides a way across a very steep wall. Traverse this to a juniper ledge, and continue up to the left but not too far as this leads off the rock. Move back right, to enjoy the superb rough rocks of the buttress front. String the rocky bits together till they end at a junction of gullies. Cross to rocks on the left, and again a little higher, before it peters out. Cross the scree on the right and walk to the steep buttress above. The buttress provides a difficult finish. Just up the right wall of the

Scafell, South-East Side, Greencove Wyke

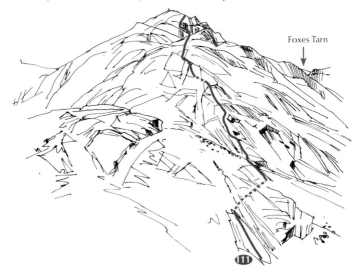

Foxes Tarn

steep rocks a gangway slants left above the steep nose. Cross this, exposed, and pull onto easy rocks on the front. The scrambling eases into walking to the broad summit ridge of Scafell.

Cam Spout, in dry conditions, with the South-East Side of Scafell behind

231

112. Cam Spout Crag

Grade 1 NY215055

Cam Spout Crag is steep and grassy but a diagonal scree rake makes an obvious line. 200m of height is gained.

The route described provides an unusual but toilsome way onto the Scafell ridge.

Approach: From the path below the crags gain the left-hand side of the rocks.

Route: Some preliminary mossy rocks can be climbed to gain the start of the diagonal rake. This proves to be of scree, but the toil can be minimised by keeping to the right edge. It ends on the brink of a dramatic overhanging drop into Peregrine Gully, the impressive but loose rift which is a prominent feature of the crag. Scramble up the exposed edge of the buttress above. At a steepening bear left until the edge can be regained. Finish up a shattered ridge.

Cam Spout and Tom Fox's Crag

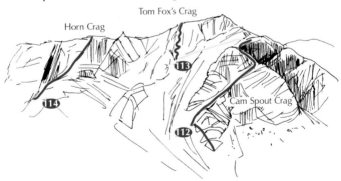

Tom Fox's Crag

Horn Crag

Cam Spout Crag

113. Tom Fox's Crag

Grade 2 NY212055

This little frequented combe lies above and behind Cam Spout Crag. A cirque of crags above steep screes rims its edge. A special visit would be excessively toilsome, but it provides a logical scrambling continuation to Cam Spout Crag (Route 112), although this is more serious.

Approach: From the easy-angled ridge above Cam Spout Crag, traverse below the first crag to the left end of the second, to reach a gully amongst slabs.

Route: Climb a short mossy wall into the gully then take to rocks on its right. A zigzag route avoids difficulties then continues up a fine rock tower which develops into a spiky arête.

The summit of Slight Side lies just to the left and a short diagonal descent could incorporate the following route.

Lonely and serious, **a mountaineering scramble for the competent**. You need to take care on the rock. 100m of height is gained.

114. Horn Crag, Slight Side

Grade 2 NY212048

Slight Side is the southernmost outlier of the Scafell range, though rarely visited for its own sake, it has a fine rocky summit – a prominent pyramid which commands extensive views. The eastern side of the mountain is the last rampart of the very craggy barrier stretching from above Cam Spout Crag.

The scramble is described with an Upper Eskdale approach as it is a logical continuation to the Esk Gorge scramble (Route 106), although Scale Gill (Route 105) would be an equally good alternative approach.

Solid, rough rock-scrambling on a broad buttress. Although the scrambling is easy it is **exposed, with a big crag atmosphere**, and although the basic rock is good the ledges are strewn with loose stones. Care is required. 100m of height is gained.

Approach: From the top of the Esk Gorge bear left up easy-angled grass slopes. A tongue of grass between scree slopes reaches to the lowest crags of Horn Crag which is the prominent buttress directly below the summit. From Scale Beck join the path along the upland shelf to Upper Eskdale. Take the higher path past High Scarth Crag to Silverybield Crag just above the path. A scramble up the broken rocks, avoiding a steep wall, could be incorporated. Soon after this Horn Crag is seen on the left.

Route: Start at the lowest pink rocks just left of the scree. Scramble into a recess, cross to a spiky rib on the right and go up to a scree shelf. Cross left to another spiky rib, climb it on its left side and continue until it develops into a scree ramp. Do not follow this, but for more interest bear right onto the good rocks of the exposed buttress front. Cross the now grassy ramp to a rock wall. Climb just left of a crack to gain a mossy slab and the edge overlooking the ramp. Continue to a steep wall, climbed on big holds in its centre by a right to left ascent. Scramble by the left side of a cleft to finish.

Horn Crag

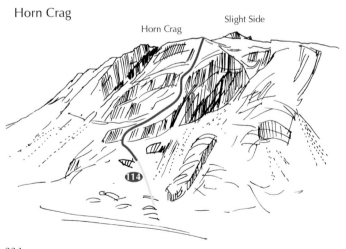

The top is a few hundred yards further. Finish with a flourish up the summit slabs. A cairned descent path lies to the south of the crags.

115. Thor's Buttress and Pen

Grade 3★★★ *NY224065*

Upper Eskdale beyond the Great Moss is a wild sanctuary which requires some effort to reach. The steep, clean pillar of Esk Buttress (shown as Dow Crag on OS maps) has some classic rock climbs. A little further on its right is the more amenable Thor's Buttress with the rock peak of Pen just above. Thor's Cave is the dark gash with a corner crack to its left. Left again are easier angled rocks, clean and rough, and it is up this that our scramble winds a way. The buttress tails into grass with the summit rocks of Pen above. The whole is an extremely good outing, with strong character and interest.

Airy scrambling, steep at first, **some route-finding ability required**. 100m of height is gained on Thor's Buttress, and 50m on Pen.

Approach: Park near Brotherilkeld and make a long walk up the valley past the Great Moss and the foot of Esk Buttress. This takes about 2 hours. An alternative approach is via Mosedale and across the low intervening ridge into upper Eskdale.

Route: Start at the lowest rocks where two scree shoots merge, and scramble up mossy rocks to a grass terrace below the corner crack. Follow the well-trodden route rising left onto the front of the buttress. Zigzag up the easiest way and follow a ramp back right to reach the prominent overhanging flakes on the left of the main corner crack. Climb a grassy gully at the side of the flakes. Move back left behind the topmost flake and traverse a long bilberry ledge to its end. Make a short steep ascent with an energetic pull onto the top of a block.

Easier walls and ledges trend right to overlook the gully. You are faced with a smooth slabby section with

Thor's Buttress, topped by the rock cone of Pen

Thor's Buttress and Pen

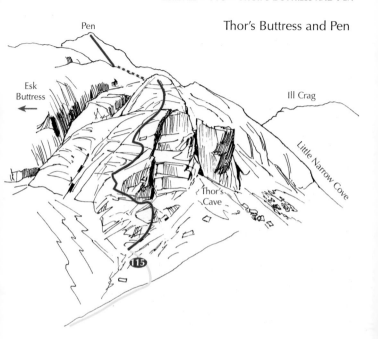

a prominent boulder flake perched on the slab. Go left under a boulder flake to a bilberry ledge and along for 10m to where the wall is less steep. A mossy scoop with good holds proves the key. Easier ground above is followed again to the right edge above the gully. A fine rib is climbed by a steep groove 6m left of an un-stable looking perched block. The buttress merges into the hillside.

It is possible to leave the scramble here and traverse right, across Little Narrowcove to the start of Ill Crag (Route 116) scramble.

Well above are the summit rocks of **Pen**, a finely shaped rock peak. Plod up steep grass to the rocks which are

Scrambling on the rough slabs of Ill Crag, South-East Face

guarded by a steep wall. Walk left to climb a corner groove which ascends the full height to the summit.

The scramble can be prolonged by a further two rock tiers then a long walk to the summit of Scafell Pike, but Pen is well worth a visit for its own sake. Or descend with care into Little Narrowcove where the following scramble (Route 116) can be climbed.

116. South-East Face, Ill Crag

Grade 3 or 2★★★ NY226068

With a vertical height of 300 metres, this is one of Lakeland's longest scrambles, and must be the finest way to reach the summit of the mountain. In detail, the face is more a broken mountainside composed of areas of crag, scree and grass. The route described below is of great interest with long stretches of continuous scrambling on excellent rock. Route-finding ability is necessary and whilst it is possible to avoid crucial sections, once embarked upon them, they are quite sustained, serious and inescapable. Avoidance reduces the standard but not the interest. This route is highly recommended to competent scramblers with experience of rock climbing. Don't worry if you lose the described way, many people return and take a different, equally enjoyable route each time.

Approach: Make a long approach up Eskdale (over 2 hours), or from Borrowdale over Esk Hause. The finest approach is by the Esk Gorge then follow the path close to the river into the upper valley. Pass the steep crag of

A long mountaineering route, mainly slab climbing on excellent rock until the upper buttress, which provides a steep and serious, though avoidable, finish. **A rope is advised** for the grade 3 Central Slabs and the steep Upper Buttress.

Ill Crag

Ill Crag

Little Narrow Cove

116

117

Ⓒ Central Slabs
Ⓤ Upper Buttress

Esk Buttress and the adjacent Thor's Buttress scramble to reach the narrow side valley of Little Narrowcove. Climb the steep right spur of this to reach the lowest slabs. The face is really the north-east flank of Little Narrowcove. There are two areas of continuous crag on either side of a more broken central area, which includes a prominent clean slab above a slightly overhanging prow of rock. Our route takes the slabby central area, approaching by a devious but intriguing line, which starts at slabs near the foot of the face.

Route: Start at the lowest slabs, left of and a little higher than a mossy side wall.

First section – to the Central Slabs

Climb pleasant clean slabs to a ledge, then the steeper slab above, either by a groove on its left edge or a more devious route starting on the left and crossing a central groove to finish up the right-hand slab. Now there is an area of easier slabs. Note the slightly overhanging prow above. You are aiming to reach the clean rocks on its right at a lower level. After the easy slabs walk right across grass to reach another area of clean rocks above a steep little mossy wall. Attain this by a bilberry chute. At the top move left carefully avoiding a large flake, onto a narrow grey rib. This ends in a grassy bay below the steep wall (there is an impressive block directly above). Climb the clean buttress on the right of this, first by a clean steep nose to a heather recess. Leave this by a groove on the right then follow a rake just on the left of the buttress crest. Finish by an awkward mossy slab. The crest of the buttress is now on the right and a slab above leads to a grass terrace below the sweep of the Central Slabs.

Second section – the Central Slabs

If these slabs were more easily accessible they would sport some popular rock climbs in their own right. As they are but one part of our overall route it is necessary to have to find a scrambling route up them. The easiest ways (Grade 2) avoid the main, smooth slab by going to the right then

Complex route-finding to seek the best stretches of interesting clean rock.

A rope and steady leader are required for the grade 3 slab route.

back left. The grade 3 route described below is technically quite easy rock climbing (easier than appearances suggest), but it requires a long runout of rope to reach the top. The slabs together reach about 48m in height.

The clean central sweep of slab is bounded on its left by a heathery groove. Aim to reach this groove and continue up the left edge of the slabs. Start in the centre of the slab and climb for 6m until ledges lead towards the heather groove. Ascend the rocks on the immediate right of the groove, crossing the groove at its top under a flake crack to gain the edge of the buttress. Move back right and continue up the crest of the rib. A short wall brings the upper buttress into view. Cross screes on the left to a clean steep wall, which you climb first on large flakes near the right end, followed by easier ribs.

Third section – the Upper Buttress

On the upper buttress is a deep, mossy v-gully. Right of this and at a lower level is a nose. Right again is a more broken, easier rib providing a viable grade 2 alternative to the more difficult grade 3 route as follows.

Head towards the v-gully then go across to a pedestal on the right. From here make an exposed traverse of the nose and head up the edge to easier ground. Now cross a grassy gully to reach the fine buttress on its left. Gain the buttress and follow the edge until it steepens. Good holds are used to gain a little height. Move left into a groove and up to a ledge on the right. Go straight ahead on good holds for 6m, then move up and left on small but good holds to reach the left edge of the rib and follow easier rock to the top.

The exposed upper buttress of the grade 3 route involves rock climbing and **a rope is strongly advised of the grade 3 route**.

Fourth section – the final slopes

A short grass slope rightwards leads to a clean rock rib which provides a pleasant stairway between large screes, eventually merging into large boulders which finish abruptly at the summit.

Easy scrambling completes the route.

Scafell Pike is an obvious continuation with the option of bagging Scafell by Broad Stand before returning to Eskdale either by Slight Side or Cam Spout.

117. Cockly Pike Ridge, Ill Crag

Grade 1★★ NY228070

A combination of walking and easy scrambling over a succession of rocky knolls starting close to the valley floor finishes some 400m higher at the summit. Beware of loose stones on ledges.

This route takes the right-hand skyline of Ill Crag as seen from Eskdale. It is a long mountaineering scramble with no route-finding problems that requires less commitment than Route 116.

Approach: A long walk up Eskdale from Brotherilkeld gains the remote upper valley. Go past the side valley of Little Narrowcove to where the path takes the crest of a small moraine. Cross the boulder slope on the left to the first rocks. This point can also be reached from Borrowdale or Langdale, by way of Esk Hause, dropping down the head of Eskdale to the start of the route.

Route: Climb the first knoll by rocks on its left, then a succession of similar rock pyramids. Keep to the pleasantest, cleanest areas of sound rock and take care with loose flakes. At one point move back left above a steep, mossy barrier and so reach the top of Cockly Pike. Opposite is a barrier. Cross this by a grass rake on its left and keep to the best rocks, steep at first. Cross a dip and keep to rocks on the left followed by a chaos of huge boulders. Go left again, across a scree shoot and along a grass terrace to reach a good clean rib. A mossy slab slants right. This can be followed to its top then head left to regain the best rock. Or with more difficulty, break out up the steep left wall and up to the bounding rib. The jumble of rock continues, keep left to reach a good clean sweep which terminates in a levelling where the next stage can be seen. This is a steep scree covered hillside, but in between the scree, find clean rock ribs which prolong the scrambling. An obvious rib gives very pleasant sport before merging into larger scree. Bear left to reach solid rock again and stable boulders to reach the skyline. Finally, there is a good finish on a tower of superb rock to a summit. The mountain's true summit is close by.

Esk Hause is easily reached for a return to Borrowdale, or continue over Scafell Pike to Mickledore for a return to Eskdale. The very fit could reach Scafell by Broad Stand (Route 22, vol. 2, Grade 3) and reach Eskdale by Slight Side.

118. Esk Pike Fortress
Grade 3* NY235066

This short, steep west-facing crag overlooking the head of Eskdale, which catches the sun, makes for a longer scramble than it first appears. The route is a useful filler after doing other scrambles in the area.

A short scramble with a 'big crag' atmosphere. Good rock. 70m of height is gained.

Approach: Reach Esk Hause from Borrowdale or Langdale and cross slopes on the Eskdale side, to below the crag. Cross a stable scree shoot to mount steeply to the foot of an easy-angled spur below the steep main crag, which here takes on the aspect of a fortress.

Route: Follow the slabby rib, then cross to the next slab right. Climb the right side of this – take care with blocks at top of groove. The various ribs and slabs merge onto a grass rake overlooking the gully. Climb up ledges, zig-zag carefully past a perched block, to where a ledge runs back right across the steep face of the crag. Gain the ledge by a short cleft. Around the corner is a broad bay of broken rocks. Climb the back of the bay. At a shelving mossy step it is perhaps safer to step left onto a square-cut ledge where progress is easier to the plateau. The summit is two craglets away. The scramble has a sporting climax

Esk Pike Fortress

on the final crag. Start at the lowest slabs on the right.
Finish up rocks left of a jutting nose.

KENTMERE

The long Kentmere valley is quite wild in its upper reaches, where Rainsborrow Crag dominates. However, the only good scrambling is on a lesser outcrop close to Kentmere village. A narrow lane runs up the valley from Staveley to Kentmere village.

Car parking

There is limited parking near the church, though at busy times a field close to the bridge before the village is often available for parking. Only local traffic is allowed on the narrow lane into the upper valley.

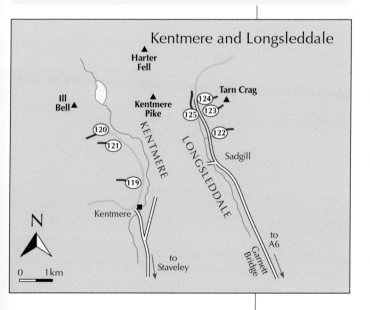

119. Raven Crag, Kentmere

*Grade 2** NY456049*

Easy scrambling on rough secure rock of excellent quality with an airy finish. Height gained is 60m.

This is the best of the many small crags which line the hillside above the road about ½ mile up the valley from Kentmere village.

Approach: From the church continue up the lane towards the Garburn Pass and head right through a gate on a surfaced lane signed 'Hartrigg'. The crag comes into view before the first cattle grid. Cross the wall directly above the grid at a stile and walk 50m left to the lowest rocks of a clean slabby spur, directly above a kink in the wall. Alternatively the kink in the wall has a stile, approached directly 30m before the cattle grid.

Route: Ascend the first rocks, bear left and climb a cleft and slabs above to finish left of a tiny tree. Ahead is a sweep of clean slabs right of tree filled gully. Start at the

Raven Crag, Kentmere

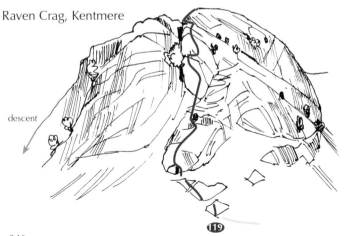

descent

119

The slabs of Raven Crag, Kentmere, give good quality scrambling

toe of the slabs and ascend using good holds; the exposure increases but it is a very pleasant long stretch of continuous rock to a grass ledge level with an oak. From the right end of the ledge follow the right edge of the slabs then move left onto slabs which lead to a spiky ridge overlooking the gully. Gain a recess on its right then finish up the steep ridge (good holds) on the left.

Descend to the neck of the spur where a track on the left drops to the intake wall.

120. East Ridge, Rainsborrow Crag
Grade 2 NY442072

The main feature of the upper valley is this huge overgrown crag of steep rock walls and bilberry covered shelves; not a good recipe for scrambling.

Approach: As for the preceding scramble, then continue along the lane, above Hartrigg, to quarries below the crag which dominates the left side of the valley. The route follows the right-hand edge of the crags, starting to the right of the last mine/quarry entrance. Approach by the stream directly above the cottages. The stream narrows into a small rock trench which can be used to enliven the way past a

From higher up the valley the route takes a striking line, but with only about 4m of rock scrambling at the start, it is disappointing. The rest is a walk in an exposed position. Height gained is 200m.

247

small cascade. Look out for the green streaks of copper ore. Well above the cascade bear left to the crags, aiming for a grass terrace just below a prominent tree in a bay.

Route: Access to the front of the buttress is barred by a steep rock wall. From the left end of the grass terrace, in an exposed position, mount a diagonal break to gain a flat ledge leading left onto the easy front. Mount a succession of bilberry shelves; it is quite airy for over 100m, then the angle lessens to allow you to walk along a narrower ridge to the gentle grassy summit of Yoke.

The ridge around the head of Kentmere makes an excellent continuation walk over Ill Bell, Froswick and Mardale Ill Bell to Nan Bield Pass, with an optional return to Kentmere village over Kentmere Pike.

121. South Gill, Rainsborrow Crag

Grade 3 NY444064

Better than it looks, but with some shattered rock and vegetation. In poor conditions **a rope is advised** to protect several short but difficult pitches and the exposed grass escape.

On the southern side of Rainsborrow Crag is a straight-cut narrow cleft which hosts a tiny stream. The route follows a basically sound quartz vein which cuts through friable rock on each side.

Approach: As for Route 120, head along the lane towards Rainsborrow Crag where the cleft can be identified on its left. Leave the road at the brow of the hill just through a gate and walk to the foot of the cleft above the fell wall.

Route: Follow the streambed to enter the cleft on the right. Several short, steep pitches prove surprisingly awkward, to culminate in a steep little fall which can only be negotiated when dry. Escape left before this by a tree onto a very steep grass slope. The ravine continues more easily above the fall.

LONGSLEDDALE

This is one of Lakeland's quieter valleys, perhaps due to the very narrow access road which demands slow, careful driving. The valley head above Sadgill is wild and rocky. Few climbers bother with the unfashionable crags for the rock is not perfect, yet Longsleddale can provide a pleasant scrambling day in sharp contrast to crowded central Lakeland.

Car parking
There is limited parking at the end of the surfaced road at Sadgill bridge. The continuation track is popular with 4x4 drivers but is too rough for normal cars.

122. Galeforth Gill

*Lower section 1 or 2**
*Upper falls Grade 4** NY484066*

The eastern side of Longsleddale above Sadgill is steep and craggy. About midway between Sadgill and Buckbarrow Crag, Galeforth Gill flows over a lip of crag in a prominent waterfall. Well worth doing as an easy scramble even if the challenge of the top falls is declined.

Approach: About ½ mile along the rough lane from Sadgill, just after a slight descent, go through a gate on the right. A prominent circular stand of trees on the hillside comes into view. Galeforth Gill is just before this.

Route: The bed becomes rocky almost immediately, with an introductory pitch at a small fall. Walking follows to the start of the main fare, where the hillside steepens and the scrambling is now almost continuous to the top of the falls. The rock stratum is vertical which results in groovy

A surprisingly continuous scramble on a good, rough rock bed. Overflow channels give a choice of route and make the gill feasible on a wet day if the flow is not too great. **Rope advised for the upper falls**, which need dry conditions. Height gain is 200m.

Good scrambling in the rocky bed of Galeforth Gill

flutings, which are quite pleasant to climb. A steep little climb just above the start leads into a narrowing with a waterchute (passable in dry conditions), alternatively cross to a recess overflow in the right wall. Regain the gill to face another small fall climbed a few feet left of the water by a V-groove.

Slabs left of the main stream are climbed by a parallel weakness to join the stream and a steep fall, ascended on the right. An easing of angle brings the top falls into view, together with a change in the lie of the rock to a more slabby structure. In wet conditions socks may be necessary. Climb the slabs left of the watercourse to a succession of rock steps in about 45m of good scrambling towards the upper falls. There is a choice of route on broad cascades. A steeper fall just below the upper falls is climbed by a right-to-left weakness onto a rising shelf below the steep final barrier.

The upper falls

The scrambling becomes much more serious and **rope protection is advised**. The main watercourse may provide a difficult pitch in dry conditions, but the route described takes the overflow channel in a V-groove left of the main stream. If wet, climb it in socks. It is steep and awkward at about 8m (nut runner) and then move right 3m to easier climbing up shelves to a tree belay in about 25m. Various possibilities lie above, but the continuation of the overflow channel is steep, mossy and lacking in holds. Better is a grassy groove directly above the tree. This is steep and an obvious jug hold on its left wall is loose. Smaller holds in the crack are solid and the finishing holds are good.

An alternative is to cross the main stream by a descending shelf to the rib on its right. Mount a shelf by the side of a large detached and apparently unstable block. Step above the block to easy ground. Yet another way, and probably the best if water conditions are favourable, is to ascend the main fall by a zigzag route starting on its right. Above the falls the scramble continues a short way before it peters out.

A slight path leads to the top of Tarn Crag where the summit crags offer more scrambling (see Route 123). Descent from the top of the falls can be made well left of the main crag by a scree and grass gully, or walk down the craggy spur of Great Howe to Sadgill.

123. Tarn Crag, Pinnacle Ribs

Grade 2★ NY484072

The rock is more difficult to climb than looks suggests, so the scrambling on this broad buttress is rather limited.

Approach: From Sadgill walk the rough valley road to just past a clump of trees within a circular wall, on the right,

After a feeble start the route improves and develops into an interesting finish. Avoid the grass and keep to the excellent rock for best sport. The height gain on the main crag is 120m; on the summit crags it is 30m.

where a gate leads onto the open fell. A diagonal ascent leads to the foot of the broken buttress, well to the right of Buckbarrow Crag at the head of the valley. To the right of the centre of the buttress, on the right of a scree cone, is a large ash tree (below a prominent square-topped pinnacle). The route starts at the tree.

Alternatively walk past the crag on the rough road to an access stile below Buckbarrow Crag where a traverse right takes you to the crag. **Access restrictions may apply during the bird-nesting season this way.**

Route: Slabs on the left of the ash are climbed to grass slopes on the left of the pinnacle. Move right to the gap behind this and climb a short, steep rib on large holds to grass and the foot of a prominent rib. Do not climb

Tarn Crag, Pinnacle Ribs

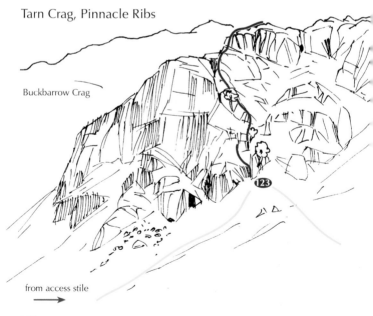

Buckbarrow Crag

from access stile

this direct; move to the easier angled rib on the right. Easy rocks lead to a grass shelf then move left to climb a fine clean rib overlooking a steep drop. Avoid a steep tower by heading over grassy rocks on its right. The route is completed by way of an excellent scramble up long, slabby ribs and a rock crest to the open fell.

Tarn Crag summit rocks

The summit rocks are seen well above and it is worth the walk up steep grassy slopes to gain this final step in the scramble. The rock buttress directly below the summit is our objective. The initial steep wall is cut by a rising gangway to the left, whence easier-angled slabs of perfect knobbly rock land almost at the huge summit cairn which poses the final ascent! The cairn and scattered timbers around it are remnants of a water authority construction.

124. Buckbarrow Crag, Left Edge

Grade 2 NY481074

The main crag of Buckbarrow carries too much vegetation for good scrambling but there is a route on the left bounding edge of the crags. **Access restrictions may apply during the bird nesting season and are noted by the access stile**.

Approach: Follow the rough road from Sadgill for 2km to a stile on the right which gives access to the crags. Make a short ascent up slopes on the left of the crag. The lower tier is bounded on its left by a greasy gully, with a rock spur on its left rising almost from the path.

Route: Scramble up the spur to the foot of a steep corner crack at the base of a spiky arête. The corner crack is a strenuous rock-climbing pitch of 6m, but can be avoided easily on its left and the ridge regained at a tree. Behind the tree the ridge narrows and becomes quite exposed, in

Not as good as the other routes around here, and the rock requires you to take great care, being composed of sharp flakes, some of which are unsound. Height gain is 110m.

The rocky head of Longsleddale

two steps to a broad terrace. The continuation of the ridge on the upper tier appears quite ferocious but proves otherwise. Gain the ridge by scree and grass ledges from left to right. Exciting, scary scrambling on huge spiky holds (great care needed to judge the safety of these) takes you to the top of the crags.

125. River Sprint

Grade 1 (with short sections of 2✱) NY478077

The rocky streambed runs in part in a slight ravine. It is only worth exploring in a dry spell.

Hardly a true gill climb, for the height gain is modest, the River Sprint runs in a rocky bed below the quarry road where it passes Buckbarrow Crag. This is a pleasant place to visit, especially if you like water-sculpted rock. There are many 'marmites' (a French word meaning 'cooking pot', which describes perfectly the shape of the water-worn basins). The bed is broad and solid, an indication of the amount of water which often flows here.

The final rock step, in the left fork, of the River Sprint

Approach: From Sadgill walk the rough road for 2km and near the base of Buckbarrow Crag take a gate on the left which gives access to the river.

Route: The walls close in to form a small ravine, guarded by a large boulder. This is easily surmounted on its left but the waterfall above is impassable although it is worth seeing before returning to the start of the ravine. Ignore an escape on the right, facing down, just above the boulder, as it difficult to regain the stream above the fall. Go lower downstream to escape on the left wall and re-enter the ravine just above the fall, where grass ledges lead into the stream. Continue up the more open streambed, with an interesting swarm across a flake which forms a little fall in mid-stream. Above is a double cascade best ascended by rocks on its left. The upper cascade is more awkward and here the rocks are slippery, making an ascent in socks advisable. Cross the left wall into a recess and escape steeply on good but slippery holds. The upper cascade can also be surmounted by superb rough rock on the wall to its right. Start fairly far right beneath a sapling then climb a few feet and traverse left to exit up a short groove.

The scramble appears to have fizzled out, but there are some good rocky bits and a fine finish up the left-hand fork, up rocks on the left of a steep little fall.

THE HOWGILL FELLS

Although strictly speaking not part of the Lake District, the following trip is worthy of inclusion. The Howgill Fells are the smooth, rounded hills to the east of the M6 south of Tebay.

126. Black Force and Carlingill

Grade 1✴ SD644992

Carlingill is a short, deeply incised valley amongst the smoothly steep grassy slopes of the Howgill Fells. It runs a westerly course to join the River Lune three miles below Tebay, where the Lune Gorge is at its most beautiful. Travellers on the nearby motorway are mostly unaware that hidden behind a shoulder of Fell Head is a quiet, remote valley which forms an excellent starting point for a walk on these beautifully formed, velvet-like hills. **Access restrictions may apply during bird nesting season.**

Approach: After leaving the M6 at J38 (Tebay) turn south on the A685 driving through the village for two miles to Low Borrowbridge, then take a minor road on the eastern side of the valley for a mile and park shortly after the stream of Carlingill. Slight paths lead into the valley. Take the right-hand fork and round the corner the charm of the valley is felt. Even the drone of the motorway is muffled. The flat-bottomed valley changes to a more exciting V-shape as the sides close in. After a preliminary scramble in the streambed the side stream of Black Force enters on the right.

An ascent of an impressive ravine, avoiding falls by easy detours. The rock is a mixture of shales and slates; far from ideal for climbing but acceptable if cautious. The eroded exit needs particular care. Height gain is 140m.

Route: The first step in the stream is taken direct, then walk up right to a steepening hollow of rock and vegetation. There is an exposed step back left overlooking the stream, or avoid this by a detour further right. The green hued pools are delightful. An easy bouldery walk up a deep ravine gains the upper amphitheatre with an impressive smooth slab on its right wall. The stream bends left and an exposed worn-rock scramble exit is made on the little ridge on its left.

As a springboard for gaining height this makes a good start to a walk on the fell tops, but for a short day a return down the upper ravine of Carlingill makes a logical round trip (described below).

Descent by Carlingill

From the top of Black Force ascend a little and bear left to a small horizontal track which enables the flat col at the head of Carlingill to be reached. Follow the gill down as it cuts a ravine to the head of an impressive fall. There is no direct descent here. Climb up out of the gill a few metres to a small platform on the right edge (looking down) and make a rather exposed traverse along a tiny track, just above rock slabs, to reach a steep grassy rib, a descent of which drops into the gill below the fall. After this it is scrambly walking along the base of a deep V-shaped ravine back to the foot of Black Force.

Whilst in the Howgills, mention must be made of that other impressive ravine on the eastern side of the hills, **Cautley Spout**. Impressive to look at, Cautley Spout is a well known and popular waterfall. It is possible to scramble easily up the streambed to have a close look at the main fall but no further. The cascades above the main fall are over atrocious shale and slippery rock and are not recommended for scrambling.

APPENDIX 1
Route Index (alphabetical)

(Note: entries are listed both by scramble route and by crag where appropriate)

Route	Grade	Stars	Page
Crinkle Crags Buttress	1		94
Crinkle Gill	1	*	93
Crook Crag by Great Whinscale	2	**	209
Dow Crag, Easter Gully and Intermediate Gully	4		162
Dow Crag, Easy Terrace and its continuation	3	***	159
Dow Crag, E-Buttress	4	*	162
Dow Crag, F-Buttress	4		163
Dungeon Ghyll, Lower section	1	*	47
Dungeon Ghyll, Upper ravine	3	*	49
E-Buttress, Dow Crag	4	*	162
Easedale Gill	1	*	100
East Rib, Tarn Crag	2	*	56
East Ridge, Harrison Stickle	1 or 2	*	75
East Ridge, Rainsborrow Crag	2		247
Easter Gully and Intermediate Gully, Dow Crag	4		162
Easy Terrace, Dow Crag	3	***	159
Esk Gorge	2	***	219
Esk Pike Fortress	3	*	243
Esk Pike, North West Spur	2		88
F-Buttress, Dow Crag	4		163
Far Hill Crag	2	**	180
Galeforth Gill, Lower section	1 or 2	**	249
Galeforth Gill, Upper falls	4	**	251
Gibson Knott, Horn Crag, Route 1	3		103
Gill Cove Crag, North Edge	2		117
Gimmer Crag, South-East Gully	2	*	46
Glassy Crag	2		147
Glassy Crag Continuation Ribs	2		149
Goat Crag, Coniston Old Man	1		155
Great Blake Rigg	3	**	181
Great Carrs Buttress	2	**	153
Great Carrs, Central Buttress	2	*	154
Great Gill	2	*	223
Great How	3	**	124
Green Crag, West Side	1 or 2	**	213
Grey Band Route, Pike of Stickle	4	**	79
The Groove, Tarn Crag	3	*	54
Hardknott Gill	1		193

APPENDIX 2
Route Index (by star grading)

Route	Grade	Page
3 Stars		
Gills		
Esk Gorge	2	219
Crags		
Crescent Climb, Pavey Ark	4	68
Easy Terrace, Dow Crag	3	159
Ill Crag, South-East Face	2 or 3	239
Jack's Rake, Pavey Ark	1	64
Long Crag Buttress	1	125
Pike of Stickle, Main Face	3	77
Raven Crag, Yewdale	2	139
Thor's Buttress and Pen	3	235
2 Stars		
Gills		
Cam Spout	3	227
Galeforth Gill, Lower Section	1 or 2	249
Galeforth Gill, Upper Falls	4	251
Lingcove Beck	2	226
Low Birker Force	3	206
Scale Gill (Cowcove Beck)	2	217
Stake Gill	1 or 2	82
Stickle Gill	1	52
Tarn Beck	1 or 2	167
Crags		
The Bell	1	105
Belles Knott	2	101
Brandy Crag, Harter Fell	2 or 3	188
Brim Fell Slabs	2	111
Cockly Pike Ridge, Ill Crag	1	242

Route	Grade	Page
Borlase Crags, Route 2	3	147
Bowfell Links, Pinnacle Rib	1	85
Castle How	2	191
Cove Rib	3	119
Dow Crag, E-Buttress	4	162
East Rib, Tarn Crag	2	56
East Ridge, Harrison Stickle	1 or 2	75
Esk Pike Fortress	3	243
Great Carrs, Central Buttress	2	154
The Groove, Tarn Crag	3	54
Harter Beanie	2	205
Harter Fell, North-West Crags	2	201
High Wether Crag	2	137
Little How	2 or 3	122
Loft Crag Buttress	2	45
Long Crag, Boulder Route	2	128
Long Crag, Wetherlam	1 or 2	150
Long Scar, Old Holborn	2	95
Low Wether Crag	3	136
Lower Hows	2	135
Pavey Far East	2	67
Pike of Stickle, West Gully Ribs	3	81
Pussie's Paradise	2	143
Raven Crag, Langdale	2	42
Raven Nest How	2	178
Raven Tor	4	120
Red How from Wrynose Bottoms	1 or 2	199
Scafell, South-East Side, Greencove Wyke	3	229
Scrambler's Corner, Black Crag, Pike of Blisco	2	96
Shudderstone How and Near Hill Crag	2	175
Simon's Nick Ridge	3	115
Sourmilk Gill, Easedale	1	100
South-East Gully, Gimmer	2	46
The Spur, Tarn Crag	2	55
Swallow Scar	2	145
Tarn Crag, Pinnacle Ribs	2	251
Thorn Crag	1 or 2	44

LISTING OF CICERONE GUIDES

Roads and Tracks of the
  Lake District
Rocky Rambler's Wild Walks
Scrambles in the Lake District
  North
  South
Short Walks in Lakeland
  1 South Lakeland
  2 North Lakeland
  3 West Lakeland
The Cumbria Coastal Way
The Cumbria Way and the
  Allerdale Ramble
The Lake District
  Anglers' Guide
Tour of the Lake District

DERBYSHIRE, PEAK DISTRICT AND MIDLANDS

High Peak Walks
The Star Family Walks
Walking in Derbyshire
White Peak Walks
  The Northern Dales
  The Southern Dales

SOUTHERN ENGLAND

A Walker's Guide to the
  Isle of Wight
London – The definitive
  walking guide
The Cotswold Way
The Greater Ridgeway
The Lea Valley Walk
The North Downs Way
The South Downs Way
The South West Coast Path
The Thames Path
Walking in Bedfordshire
Walking in Berkshire
Walking in Buckinghamshire
Walking in Kent
Walking in Sussex
Walking in the Isles of Scilly
Walking in the
  Thames Valley
Walking on Dartmoor
Walking on Guernsey
Walking on Jersey
Walks in the South Downs
  National Park

WALES AND WELSH BORDERS

Backpacker's Britain
  Wales
Glyndwr's Way
Great Mountain Days
  in Snowdonia
Hillwalking in Snowdonia
Hillwalking in Wales
  Vols 1 and 2
Offa's Dyke Path
Ridges of Snowdonia
Scrambles in Snowdonia
The Ascent of Snowdon
The Lleyn Peninsula
  Coastal Path
The Pembrokeshire
  Coastal Path
The Shropshire Hills
The Spirit Paths of Wales
Walking in Pembrokeshire
Walking on the
  Brecon Beacons
Welsh Winter Climbs

INTERNATIONAL CHALLENGES, COLLECTIONS AND ACTIVITIES

Canyoning
Europe's High Points

EUROPEAN CYCLING

Cycle Touring in France
Cycle Touring in Ireland
Cycle Touring in Spain
Cycle Touring in Switzerland
Cycling in the French Alps
Cycling the Canal du Midi
Cycling the River Loire
The Danube Cycleway
The Grand Traverse of the
  Massif Central
The Way of St James

AFRICA

Climbing in the Moroccan
  Anti-Atlas
Kilimanjaro: A Complete
  Trekker's Guide
Mountaineering in the
  Moroccan High Atlas
Trekking in the
  Atlas Mountains
Walking in the Drakensberg

ALPS – CROSS-BORDER ROUTES

100 Hut Walks in the Alps
Across the Eastern Alps: E5
Alpine Ski Mountaineering
  1 Western Alps
  2 Central and Eastern Alps
Chamonix to Zermatt
Snowshoeing
Tour of Mont Blanc
Tour of Monte Rosa
Tour of the Matterhorn
Trekking in the Alps
Walking in the Alps
Walks and Treks in the
  Maritime Alps

PYRENEES AND FRANCE/SPAIN CROSS-BORDER ROUTES

Rock Climbs In The Pyrenees
The GR10 Trail
The Mountains of Andorra
The Pyrenean Haute Route
The Pyrenees
The Way of St James
  France
  Spain
Through the Spanish
  Pyrenees: GR11
Walks and Climbs in
  the Pyrenees

AUSTRIA

Trekking in Austria's
  Hohe Tauern
Trekking in the Stubai Alps
Trekking in the Zillertal Alps
Walking in Austria

EASTERN EUROPE

The High Tatras
The Mountains of Romania
Walking in Bulgaria's
  National Parks
Walking in Hungary

FRANCE

Ecrins National Park
GR20: Corsica
Mont Blanc Walks
The Cathar Way
The GR5 Trail

The Robert Louis Stevenson Trail
Tour of the Oisans: The GR54
Tour of the Queyras
Tour of the Vanoise
Trekking in the Vosges and Jura
Vanoise Ski Touring
Walking in Provence
Walking in the Cathar Region
Walking in the Cevennes
Walking in the Dordogne
Walking in the Haute Savoie North and South
Walking in the Languedoc
Walking in the Tarentaise and Beaufortain Alps
Walking on Corsica

GERMANY

Germany's Romantic Road
Walking in the Bavarian Alps
Walking in the Harz Mountains
Walking the River Rhine Trail

HIMALAYA

Annapurna: A Trekker's Guide
Bhutan
Everest: A Trekker's Guide
Garhwal and Kumaon: A Trekker's and Visitor's Guide
Kangchenjunga: A Trekker's Guide
Langtang with Gosainkund and Helambu: A Trekker's Guide
Manaslu: A Trekker's Guide
The Mount Kailash Trek

IRELAND

Irish Coastal Walks
The Irish Coast to Coast Walk
The Mountains of Ireland

ITALY

Gran Paradiso
Italy's Sibillini National Park
Shorter Walks in the Dolomites
Through the Italian Alps
Trekking in the Apennines
Trekking in the Dolomites
Via Ferratas of the Italian Dolomites: Vols 1 and 2
Walking in Sicily
Walking in the Central Italian Alps
Walking in the Dolomites
Walking in Tuscany
Walking on the Amalfi Coast

MEDITERRANEAN

Jordan – Walks, Treks, Caves, Climbs and Canyons
The Ala Dag
The High Mountains of Crete
The Mountains of Greece
Treks and Climbs in Wadi Rum, Jordan
Walking in Malta
Western Crete

NORTH AMERICA

British Columbia
The Grand Canyon
The John Muir Trail
The Pacific Crest Trail

SOUTH AMERICA

Aconcagua and the Southern Andes
Torres del Paine

SCANDINAVIA

Trekking in Greenland
Walking in Norway

SLOVENIA, CROATIA AND MONTENEGRO

The Julian Alps of Slovenia
The Mountains of Montenegro
Trekking in Slovenia
Walking in Croatia

SPAIN AND PORTUGAL

Costa Blanca Walks
  1 West
  2 East
Mountain Walking in Southern Catalunya
The Mountains of Central Spain
Trekking through Mallorca
Via de la Plata
Walking in Madeira
Walking in Mallorca
Walking in the Algarve
Walking in the Canary Islands
  2 East
Walking in the Cordillera Cantabrica
Walking in the Sierra Nevada
Walking on La Gomera and El Hierro
Walking on La Palma
Walking the GR7 in Andalucia
Walks and Climbs in the Picos de Europa

SWITZERLAND

Alpine Pass Route
Central Switzerland
The Bernese Alps
Tour of the Jungfrau Region
Walking in the Valais
Walking in Ticino
Walks in the Engadine

TECHNIQUES

Geocaching in the UK
Indoor Climbing
Lightweight Camping
Map and Compass
Mountain Weather
Moveable Feasts
Rock Climbing
Sport Climbing
The Book of the Bivvy
The Hillwalker's Guide to Mountaineering
The Hillwalker's Manual

MINI GUIDES

Avalanche!
Navigating with a GPS
Navigation
Pocket First Aid and Wilderness Medicine
Snow

For full and up-to-date information on our ever-expanding list of guides, visit our website: **www.cicerone.co.uk**.

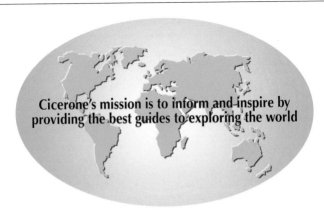

Cicerone's mission is to inform and inspire by providing the best guides to exploring the world

Since its foundation 40 years ago, Cicerone has specialised in publishing guidebooks and has built a reputation for quality and reliability. It now publishes nearly 300 guides to the major destinations for outdoor enthusiasts, including Europe, UK and the rest of the world.

Written by leading and committed specialists, Cicerone guides are recognised as the most authoritative. They are full of information, maps and illustrations so that the user can plan and complete a successful and safe trip or expedition – be it a long face climb, a walk over Lakeland fells, an alpine cycling tour, a Himalayan trek or a ramble in the countryside.

With a thorough introduction to assist planning, clear diagrams, maps and colour photographs to illustrate the terrain and route, and accurate and detailed text, Cicerone guides are designed for ease of use and access to the information.

If the facts on the ground change, or there is any aspect of a guide that you think we can improve, we are always delighted to hear from you.

Cicerone Press
2 Police Square Milnthorpe Cumbria LA7 7PY
Tel: 015395 62069 Fax: 015395 63417
info@cicerone.co.uk www.cicerone.co.uk

CICERONE